THE OFFICIAL
PRICE GUIDE
HOLIDAY
COLLECTIBLES

THE OFFICIAL®
PRICE GUIDE
HOLIDAY
COLLECTIBLES

Helaine Fendelman & Jeri Schwartz

FIRST EDITION

House of Collectibles • New York

Important Notice. All of the information, including valuations, in this book has been compiled from the most reliable sources, and every effort has been made to eliminate errors and questionable data. Nevertheless, the possibility of error, in a work of such immense scope, always exists. The publisher will not be held responsible for losses which may occur in the purchase, sale, or other transaction of items because of information contained herein. Readers who feel they have discovered errors are invited to *write* and inform us, so they may be corrected in subsequent editions. Those seeking further information on the topics covered in this book are advised to refer to the complete line of *Official Price Guides* published by the House of Collectibles.

Published by: House of Collectibles
201 East 50th Street
New York, New York 10022

Distributed by Ballantine Books, a division of Random House, Inc., New York, and simultaneously in Canada by Random House of Canada Limited, Toronto.

Text design by Holly Johnson

Part title design by Philip Draggan

Manufactured in the United States of America

ISBN: 0-876-37818-1

First Edition: October 1991

10 9 8 7 6 5 4 3 2 1

Contents

Acknowledgments

We gratefully acknowledge the assistance of the following people in preparing this book: Scott Anderson; Mark Anderton of Collector's Auction Services; Laura Beach of *The Newtown Bee*; Caroline Birenbaum of Swann Galleries; Chip Cable of Collector's Auction Services; Bob Cahn, The Primitive Man; Kim Cameron of Theriault's Auctions; Ginny Caputo and James Maxwell; Margaret Scott Carter; Sallie and Bob Connelly; Terry and Joe Dziadul; Rufus Foshee; Todd Foster; Kathleen Gips; Donald Gray of Sandwich Auction House; Harriet Green; Jim Haggenblah of Glass-Works Auctions; Kathy and Burt Hem; Sarah Himmel of Robert Skinner Auctions; Kyle Husfloen of *The Antique Trader Weekly*; Rochelle and Peter Kassai; Larry Kemper of Pettigrew Auction Gallery; Joan and Allan Lehner; Don Mehrer; Chuck Muller of *Antique Review*; Joan Pappas of Knotty Pine Antiques Market; Tom Porter of Garth's Auctions; Nancy Rosin; Pam and Chris Russell; Mary and Bob Schneider; Barb and Dick Shilvock of Calico Cat Antiques; Grand Sterling; Nancy and Bruce Thompson; Ray Turner of *The Antique Gazette*; and Lou Zimet. Special thanks to Linda Grande for all her efforts and good work and to Susan Lipschutz for photography. Our families, including Barton, Burton, Debbie, and Jonathon, deserve a special thank you for all of their help.

Introduction

This book is an overview of the rapidly developing market in holiday decorations, ornaments, and favors. For many, collecting in this area seems to be an attempt to recapture the essence of youth, family reunions, and remembered joys. There is a renewed mystique and nostalgia for articles from the past in that holidays and their decorations, especially those which were passed from generation to generation, engender a warm feeling for bygone days.

In addition, since the costs of most antiques, including eighteenth- and nineteenth-century furniture, glass, china, silver, and paintings, have escalated beyond the means of the average collector, discovering new areas of collecting is a challenge. The scarcity of such rare antique items has stimulated dealers and collectors to continue searching for objects previously ignored. Holiday items, usually made in small sizes, are also able to be displayed easily in a small space.

Within the past ten years, dealers and savvy collectors began uncovering unusual ornaments, decorations, and party favors at tag sales and flea markets. One or two dealers and trend-setting buyers began to form collections and develop expertise about these novelties. Pieces began to appear at small auction houses throughout the country. Specialized auctions and shows eventually became prevalent. New research, publications, auctions, and specialized shows have stimulated interest in holiday memorabilia.

Information and prices for this book were gathered from auction catalogs, antiques trade publications, flea markets, and antiques shows. Dimensions were given if they were listed in the sales catalogs. Values are for items in pristine condition, unless otherwise mentioned.

Even as knowledge about the objects has increased and their prices have escalated, it is still possible to find wonderful and affordable examples of these artistically designed pieces at tag sales, flea markets, antiques malls and centers, auctions, and antiques shows. We hope that this book will help you build a collection that will make your holiday celebrations even happier!

Holiday Collectibles

New Year's Day

The Romans, in 153 B.C., were the first to celebrate the holiday. They believed that, commencing on the first day of January, each person's life would begin with a clean slate, that the previous year's events would be erased, and that this day signaled a fresh beginning.

In earlier times, evil spirits were thought to be everywhere. To ban them from entering the new year, it was common to create a ruckus by ringing church bells. From this comes the expression "to ring in the New Year." By the late nineteenth century a carnival atmosphere prevailed with much drinking and noises from bells, whistles, and horns used to celebrate. At this time, also, the New Year's Day open house came into favor with the serving of eggnog, punch, and New Year's cakes. The symbols of the New Year's Baby and the gray-bearded Father Time, depicted as the old year bearing a scythe and reminding one of the death of the old year, also became popular at this time.

Today celebratory parties continue. They begin the night before with New Year's Eve cocktail parties and dinner dances. On New Year's Day, the Mummer's parade in Philadelphia and the Rose Bowl parade in Pasadena, California, have become traditional events along with numerous football games and open-house parties.

Late Victorian decorations, primarily for parties at home, included cardboard candy containers, silver foil banners proclaiming "Happy New Year," calling cards used by well-bred ladies and gentlemen and left as reminders of their visit, postcards, and greeting cards. At the turn of the twentieth century, honeycomb paper balls were hung about the house. Printed handkerchiefs and Berlin work mottoes with New Year's motifs were also made during this era.

Most of the collectible decorations are from the 1920s, '30s, and '40s. Noisemakers include lithographed tin horns, bells, clackers, clappers, and cardboard whistles with feather blow-outs. For the party table, paper companies, with the Dennison Co. being the major producer, manufactured paper plates, cups, and napkins imprinted with New Year's greetings. Paper nut cups and candy containers were available along with full-figure paper and pressed board centerpieces which duplicated the New Year's Baby and Father Time with scythe in hand. Wearing hats at

Group of early 20th-century lithographed tin noisemakers, New Year's handkerchief, and roast turkey candy container.

the New Year's party was de rigueur. Most were decorated with paper fringe, feathers, and glitter. From the latter part of the nineteenth century until the 1940s, people sent New Year's greetings by postal or greeting card. Popular motifs on the cards included the New Year's Baby ringing the bells to herald the New Year, sometimes alone or with Father Time ringing out the old year.

Late nineteenth-century needlework mottoes also included the New Year motif with brightly colored wools spelling out "Happy New Year" against a perforated paper ground. At the same time, sterling silver teaspoons were manufactured with Father Time and the words "Happy New Year" engraved in the bowl.

New Year's Day Listings

Banner, fabric, printed "Out With the Old—In With the New," 1935. ..... $22
Banner, fabric, stenciled "Auld Lang Syne," 1909, homemade, fair condition.
.... $25
Banner, paper, printed "Happy New Year," silver border, 1930. .... $10
Candy container, champagne bottle, cardboard with paper label, 1920. ..$125
Candy container, roast turkey, papier-mâché, early 20th century. $90
Centerpiece, Father Time, cardboard with scythe, embossed "New Year's Greetings," 9 inches high. $25
Centerpiece, New Year's Baby, cardboard with paper banner, "Happy New Year," early 20th century. $25
Centerpiece, top hat, black cardboard with Bakelite cane, "New Year's Greetings," 1930. .... $35
Decoration, bells, honeycomb tissue paper, white and silver. $12

Favor, champagne bottle, papier-mâché filled with confetti, early 20th century.
.... $35
Handkerchief, printed cotton, "Happy New Year Greetings" and bells, 1940.
....$5
Hat, cone shaped, crepe paper-covered cardboard, cut-out silver foil, 1928.
.... $12
Hat, glitter-covered silver headband with plume in center, 1920. .... $10
Hat, tissue paper with silver and feather band, early 20th century. $10
Invitation, Father Time, lithographed paper, package, 1930. .... $7/pkg.
Invitation, hats and noisemakers, printed cardboard, mid-20th century. $3
Menu, Fountainbleau, Miami Beach, New Year's Eve, 1957, lithographed paper.
.... $10
Menu, New Year's Day open house, handpainted with pen and ink, January 1,
1906. ....$22
Needlework, Berlin work motto, "Happy New Year," on punched paper, orig-
inal frame. $125
Noisemaker, frying pan shape, tin, with wooden balls, lithographed "New Year's
Greetings," 1930. .... $10
Noisemaker, horn, lithographed tin, New Year's Baby, red, yellow, and blue,
wooden mouthpiece, 1920. .... $10
Noisemaker, horn, paper over cardboard, silver and black, 1930. ....$5
Noisemaker, snapper, crepe paper-covered cardboard, "Happy New Year" in
glitter, early 20th century. $5
Noisemaker, whistle, blow-out, cardboard and paper, with feather blow-out,
1930. ....$5
Noisemakers, snappers, crepe paper over cardboard, multicolored gummed pa-
per labels, box, 1930. ....$35/box

Group of early 20th-century lithographed tin noisemakers,
$10–$15 each. COURTESY OF PAM AND CHRIS RUSSELL.

Photograph, New Year's Eve party, Copacabana night club, New York City, 1948, framed. $35

Photograph, Times Square, New York, New Year's Eve, 1953. .... $15

Plate, calendar, ceramic, "1910, Happy New Year," transfer cherubs. $35

Postcard, "Happy New Year," flowers encircling 1912, embossed paper. . $10

Postcard, "Happy New Year," New Year's Baby surrounded by flowers, embossed cardboard, German, early 20th century. $5

Postcard, Kewpie ringing bells, "New Year's Greetings," signed Rose O'Neill, 1910. .... $35

Spoon, demitasse, sterling silver, embossed "Happy New Year." $12

Spoon, sterling silver, cut-out New Year's Baby, early 20th century. $22

Streamer, crepe paper, printed "New Year's Greetings," mid-20th century. $5

Tablecloth, New Year's Baby and bells, printed paper, Dennison's, cellophane package, poor condition, early 20th century. .... $5/pkg.

Wall decoration, Father Time, embossed "New Year's Greetings," cardboard, early 20th century. $10

Wall decoration, flat cardboard New Year's Baby, large size. $10

Wall decoration, New Year's bells, embossed cardboard with glitter border, early 20th century. $5

Valentine's Day

The celebration of Valentine's Day stems from the martyrdom of the Christian Saint Valentine, an obscure third-century priest who was idolized for his chastity and virtue. He was believed to have been beheaded on February 14 in the year 270. On this date, certain pagan fertility rites were celebrated, and it also heralded the coming of the spring. Although once thought to be a continuation of a Roman custom of exchanging gifts, through the years the holiday evolved into a romantic event for the giving of gifts and the exchanging of handwritten, painted, and embellished notes and cards. Years and centuries later, the occasion of Saint Valentine's Day is marked by the exchanging of gifts, love tokens, and valentine cards.

In the 1700s, England became the first country to produce cards for a retail market. By the latter part of the eighteenth century, gifts were abandoned in favor of handmade letters and notes. Many of the romantics looked to books of verse for lovers and from these derived messages of affection for inclusion in the hand-decorated notes. The best examples feature symbols commonly known to the romantics and include Cupids, hearts, and handpainted, pinpricked or decoupage work.

At the end of the eighteenth century, embossed note papers with decorative borders were introduced. Even though these were extraordinarily expensive to produce, they were used extensively in England and on the Continent. By the turn of the nineteenth century, papers were embellished with colorful printed floral motifs, often encompassing cherubs. Many were engraved and later handcolored. Also at this time, perforated papers in imitation of lace began to be produced in England. The printed paper market continued to expand.

Commercial valentines on a major scale were introduced in the first quarter of the nineteenth century by Dobbs & Co. A prominent paper manufacturer in London, England, Dobbs was renowned for the quality and wide range of designs they offered. When embossed papers were used by the company, the Dobbs name was usually located near the borders. Valentine cards by this firm are eagerly sought because they exhibited extensive embossed detailing. This firm was also well known for producing a lacy effect on the decorative paper frills, sometimes even in layers.

*Mid-19th-century
embossed valentine with
paper lace surround.*
COURTESY OF NANCY ROSIN.

*Mid-19th-century
valentine.* COURTESY
OF NANCY ROSIN.

It was an ardent friend who sent these love tokens because, in England, the amount one paid for postage was calculated on the number and weight of the pages one sent. Using an envelope with its frilly embellishment added weight to the missive, thereby increasing postage. It is extremely rare to find valentines with matching envelopes from this period, and they are highly prized by today's collectors. By the middle of the nineteenth century, both in the United States and England, standard postal rates were introduced and valentines with matching envelopes became more popular. Before the postal service was introduced, the paper love tokens were delivered by hand or left on the doorstep by a shy lover. It is important to remember that it was also the custom to exchange valentines with relatives and family friends.

One of the most sought-after styles of valentines has the cobweb or beehive design. Intricately designed during the first half of the nineteenth century, such novel valentines were constructed by snipping the paper into threads to resemble a cobweb or beehive. A single thread could then be lifted in the center causing a beehive to appear. Underneath the web or hive was verse, handpainted floral motifs or sometimes a lock of hair from the loved one.

The best cut work and embossed valentines in England were made from 1840 until about 1860. Most valentines of this period bore handwritten or printed verse and were extremely sentimental in tone. For those who considered themselves unable to compose verse, there were numerous books from which to copy, such as *Flora's Interpreter: Or, The American Book of Flowers and Sentiments* by Mrs. Sarah Josepha Hale.

In America, as early as the middle part of the eighteenth century, sending and exchanging love letters was also the custom among the Pennsylvania German community. These brightly colored tokens were designed with hearts, verse, and, usually, with some sort of pinpricked or cut work embellishment. Another popular form was the fold-up letter or puzzle which was drawn all over both sides with verse and illustrations, and then had the corners folded into themselves to form an envelope. It was not uncommon for the valentine that formed its own envelope to be sealed with a drop of sealing wax. These examples are rare because many did not survive multiple foldings and unfoldings.

In addition to the simple valentines decorated with watercolor hearts and stars, more elaborate examples began to be made at the turn of the nineteenth century. The theorem-style valentine was made with the use of stencils and watercolor in exactly the same way theorem painting was executed on velvet. Many young girls learned this technique at dames' schools as part of their education. Puzzle valentines also made their appearance at the same time, usually in envelope form with corners folded, having handpainting and the tiniest handwritten messages on both

*Early 19th-century
American
hand-drawn watercolor
valentine.* COURTESY OF
NANCY ROSIN.

*Mid-19th-century embossed paper
lace valentine with handpainted
theorem-style motif.* COURTESY OF
NANCY ROSIN.

Lover's knot valentine.
COURTESY OF NANCY ROSIN.

sides of the paper decorated with love motifs. Oftentimes valentines were decorated with a love knot or the endless knot of love, as it was called during the eighteenth and nineteenth centuries. Many valentine messages were decorated with or referred to as love knots or rings because true love was thought to be like a ring, without an end.

The art of pinpricking, an eighteenth-century European pastime, was often combined with the watercolor decoration of the Fraktur valentine. The painted detail was pricked with pins to give a punched or embossed effect. Pinpricking was also combined with cut work, usually with an abundance of hearts in both single and double form.

Schnerenschnitte, a late eighteenth- and early nineteenth-century form of paper cutting executed primarily by the Pennsylvania Germans, required great skill and a pair of extremely sharp scissors. The paper was folded first, sometimes several times depending upon the desired size and design of the finished piece. The cut work was often very detailed, usually executed on white paper, and sometimes done in combination with watercolor. These works were often mounted on colored paper backgrounds. The best examples feature cut-outs of trees, foliage, birds, cherubs, and doves with hearts. Many of these show objects in pairs defining the unity of their love.

Handmade love tokens from the last quarter of the eighteenth or the first quarter of the nineteenth centuries were sometimes combined with the acrostic puzzle. This incorporated a poem or series of lines in which certain letters, usually the first in each line, formed a name or a message within the poem. A rebus or a riddle, composed of pictures suggesting the sound of the words or syllables that they represent, were sometimes used in valentines.

Early 19th-century Schnerenschnitte valentine. COURTESY OF NANCY ROSIN.

Hand-drawn Pennsylvania German Fraktur valentines from the early part of the nineteenth century are extremely collectible. Most are brightly colored watercolors on paper, often written in German (as were birth and wedding certificates of the same time period), and filled with a great number of motifs such as pots of flowers, tulips, hearts, birds, angels, houses, stars, and other geometric devices. The creators of these love notes were artistically rendering the symbols they saw in their everyday lives. Collage techniques were also often combined with handwritten sentiment or verse, applied cut-out flowers, leaves, ribbons, and, occasionally, mirrors. In addition, it was not unusual for handcut trails of leaves to form the borders. At this time also and into the middle of the nineteenth century, valentines were created as gifts for the local schoolteachers and choirmasters. In addition, they were given to young children as rewards of merit for learning Bible verse or excellence in school work.

Oftentimes, we think we are so modern today! However, in America in the early part of the nineteenth century, sharply worded comic verse was in style. Tender expressions of love and affection were cast aside in favor of nasty and often maliciously comic valentines. Many, crudely colored single pages or postcard styles, signaled the demise of the sentimental custom of sending love tokens. First handwritten in pen and ink and then, as their popularity increased, followed by engraved and handcolored valentines, these examples ridiculed people and occupations. No one was exempt, from the schoolmarm and the policeman to the old maid and the social climber. Some were political in content. Other names for these "comic" missives were penny dreadfuls (they sold for a penny and the designs were dreadful) and vinegar valentines. By the middle part of the nineteenth century, these were produced in great quantities by lithographed or wood block printed methods. Manufacturers included Elton & Co. in New York City and the Fisher Co. in New York, Boston, Philadelphia, and Baltimore. These were followed by George Whitney, T.W. Strong, and Charles Huestis. Civil War valentines were also produced in a biting style. At this same time, the New York Valentine Co. was producing soldier and sailor valentine packets. McLoughlin Brothers, also from New York, offered brightly colored nasty valentines, most of which were sold in the 25- to 50-cent range, quite expensive for the period.

During Victorian times, cards produced in America by Esther Howland and McLoughlin (who also made toys and games), and in England by Louis Prang and Raphael Tuck, became extremely popular. Valentine cards were embellished with die cut lithographed doves, various flowers, bow knots, swags, and lace surrounds. Exchanging cards, both homemade and store bought, seemed to reach its height of popularity at the end of the nineteenth century. Finishing schools encouraged the handpainting of cards, with many created for family members or secret swains. Some cards extolled flowery sentiments with folded tissue paper inserts which expanded into bells or petals when the card opened. Others were hold-to-light examples which depicted lovely scenes when held to window or lamp light.

In the middle part of the nineteenth century, fine valentines were created in Massachusetts by Esther Howland. At first she worked independently. When her work became extremely popular, she found it necessary to hire local women artists to help her. She and the ladies formed a cottage industry cutting and pasting the decorations for the cards. At the peak of her business, Howland sold 100,000 cards a year. Her father's illness eventually forced her to sell the company to George Whitney, whose valentines are identified by a "W" incorporated into the design. Howland's trademarks include accordian-style hinges, glazed paper wafers, and an "H" or "NEV Co.," which identified the New England Valentine Co.

From the middle to the latter part of the nineteenth century, sailors' valentines became desirable and extremely popular as mementos. Usually enclosed within a double wooden frame or case, they were made from various types and colors of shells arranged in decorative patterns, generally with a central cartouche enclosing a sentimental motto such as "Love" or "Be Mine." Originally made by sailors on voyages for their lovers at home, by the end of the nineteenth century, when they became more popular, sailors' valentines had evolved into a cottage industry in England.

In the United States in the late nineteenth century, various New England silver factories manufactured sterling silver teaspoons with the holiday motif at the top of the handle. One called "Cupid" was embossed with a cherub above a quiver; another, "Love," was decorated with a heart, an arrow, and entwined floral motifs. Originally these were sold through jewelry or silver shops.

During the latter part of the nineteenth century, German manufacturers produced tremendous quantities of lithographed and heavily embossed valentines with honeycomb paper inserts and ribbons. At the turn of the twentieth century, Germany was one of the most prolific manufacturers of multicolored lithographed valentines with lace and ribbon decoration. Children and cherubs, nosegays, bow knots, ribbon swags, and festoons combined with sugary sweet sentiments are the hallmarks of these cards. A great majority of these valentines were created with movable parts—doves had fluttering wings, shutters on windows opened, carriage wheels turned, hearts were proffered. Popular motifs of the day included the new modes of transportation: cars or horseless carriages overflowing with bouquets of flowers, paper ship valentines with children on the bows supporting swags of floral wreaths, hot air balloons with cherubs suspended from the baskets with bow knots, and airplanes with movable propellors. The best examples exhibit brilliantly colored movable parts, have multiple elements with folded honeycomb tissue paper pull-outs, and are in pristine condition. Often individually framed today, collectors and lovers of fine things prize these rarities.

Late nineteenth-century flat wax relief valentine ornaments were sometimes produced in cookie molds. The wax relief, usually in the form of a human figure, heart, and/or bird, was added to a bouquet of artificial flowers. Fastened to a heart and set under a blown glass dome, these decorations were also often used on a center table in the Victorian drawing room.

Other items of interest for the collector of valentine holiday memorabilia are found in the heart-shaped decorations used in and around the home during the early part of the twentieth century. Parties to celebrate St. Valentine's Day were common. Manufacturers of party paper goods, in both America and Germany, produced printed plates, napkins, cups, nut cups, invitations, place cards, and tablecloths. Hearts, cherubs or Cupids, flower festoons, and doves were common decorative motifs, almost always in red and white. Lacy doilies in heart form were used under cakes and also for homemade valentines. Embossed cardboard hearts suspended from red or white satin ribbons were sold to decorate the chandelier. Red and white crepe paper streamers crisscrossed the room bisected by red honeycomb tissue paper hearts in various sizes. Table centerpieces depicting full-figure cherubs holding quivers of arrows were carefully preserved from year to year. At the party table, crepe paper-covered individual nut cups bore gummed seals with valentine motifs. Pressed board and, later, cardboard heart-shaped candy containers were also made. In the 1940s, heart-shaped boxes were filled with heart-shaped candies decorated with sentimental sayings. These are still being made today.

In the schoolroom, valentine parties helped celebrate the day. Almost every classroom had a homemade or store-bought crepe paper-covered valentine letter box so that everyone in the class could post their greetings to one's fellow classmates. To aid in creating these valentines, packages of die cuts, paper lace trims, ribbons, and glitter were available in the dime store.

Following the end of World War I, there was a decline in exchanging valentine greetings in both England and America. By the beginning of World War II, however, there was a renewed interest in sending valentines.

German pewter and tin chocolate and ice cream molds were made in full-figure and multiple heart forms. Examples saying "Happy Valentine's Day" were also made. Aluminum molds for cakes and aspics became popular in the 1930s and '40s. Also at this time, Schrafft's and other candy companies offered red satin-covered heart-shaped boxes filled with their best chocolate candies. These boxes, particularly those in mint condition, are highly collectible. For the valentine collector, early twentieth-century postcards, especially those with Kewpies or Palmer Cox Brownies bearing hearts, are prized.

Some valentine collectors consider objects with heart or love motifs, sometimes made as love tokens, as complements to their collections. Among this group are Battersea boxes made in the middle part of the eighteenth century in England for holding snuff or sweetmeats. Many created in heart form, decorated with enamel on copper, have mottoes such as "Love the Giver" or "Esteem the Giver" and sell for $600 to $1,000. These boxes are difficult to find in good condition.

English pottery jugs and plaques, made in the early and middle part of the nineteenth century, were often decorated with handpainted or transfer motifs of love knots or verse, such as the "Sailor's Farewell," some with Sunderland luster decoration. Made in Leeds and Newcastle, most of the jugs are in the $800 to $1,200 range. During the early nineteenth century, wood block printed scarves and kerchiefs with heart motifs were sometimes given to young men by their admirers. These textiles, used for wrapping the sailor's clothing and other personal belongings, are quite rare, and, when they become available, average $1,000 each.

At the same time on the Continent, carved wooden spoons were given as love tokens to one's intended. The term "spooning" derives from these special gifts. Created in all sizes, most often with heart, flower or bird motifs, some were used as wall decorations and today sell for about $150. Also, during the nineteenth century when a sailor was on a whaling or other voyage which took him across the sea, he might possibly while away the hours carving a whalebone busk or corset stay with hearts, flowers, birds or other romantic motifs. The piece might then be given as a love token to his beloved. Some were rubbed with India ink after they were incised so that they became more colorful. Busks range in price from $1,000 to $2,500. Other common love tokens made in the middle of the nineteenth century were glass rolling pins that were originally filled with cologne. Usually made in Bristol, England, they were presents from a sailor to his loved one and today sell for $200 to $300.

When you are purchasing valentines, be sure to look for early watermarks, dates, paper laces embossed with makers' names incorporated into the designs, or makers' names or initials on the backs of the card. Early valentines have handpainted decoration used for decoupage. Later valentines used die cut lithographed applied work. There is an overwhelmingly large quantity of early and middle twentieth-century paper valentines. Therefore, it is a good idea to refrain from buying those

examples in foxed, stained, mutilated, folded, creased, dirty or otherwise poor condition. Wait for those in original condition. Do not hesitate
to buy if the love token is addressed or personalized; this adds to the
sentimentality of the treasure.

There is a well-known group of valentine collectors who share information: National Association of Valentine Collectors, P.O. Box 1404,
Santa Ana, CA 92702.

Valentine's Day Listings

Banner, printed paper, "Happy Valentine's Day," mid-20th century. $15
Banner, stenciled fabric with hearts and "Happy Valentine's Day," 1930s.
.... $75
Basket, cake, heart form, lithographed paper with embroidered sides. $35
Booklet, paper, Valentine recipes, Jell-O, early 20th century. $5
Booklet, recipes, color plates, Valentine, Baker's Chocolate, 1940. .... $10
Booklet, Valentine Queen of Hearts, Jell-O, early 20th century. $18
Bookmark, heart shape, sterling silver, Tiffany, 1930. .... $75
Bottle, cologne, decorated porcelain, heart shape, circa 1900, with chatelaine
chain and clip. $150
Bottle, scent, enamel over cobalt glass, heart shape, Moser, early 20th century.
.... $350
Box, Battersea, bird shape, "Love the Giver," mid-18th century, fair condition.
.... $900
Box, Battersea, heart shape, scene of fishermen, lacking some enamel, late 18th
century, crazed condition. $325
Box, heart shape, embossed silver, Continental, late 19th century. $450
Box, heart shape, hinge lid, sterling silver, beaded surround, early 20th century,
Alvin Sterling. $325
Box, pin, heart shape, celluloid, lift top, 1930. .... $24
Box, tin, lithographed, Art Nouveau, lady with hearts, circa 1910. .... $20
Box, tin, lithographed, toffee, heart surround, English, 1935. .... $10
Box, Tramp Art, heart shape, with hanger, early 20th century, 4 inches high.
.... $100
Box, Tramp Art, lift top with double hearts, wooden, some paint, early 20th
century, 12-inch length. $475
Bracelet, gold filled, expansion band, early 20th century, heart center. $15
Bracelet, sterling silver, hearts, some with enamel. $75
Bridge tallies, paper, with cherubs and ribbon tassels, set. $25/set
Buttons, heart-shaped Bakelite, card of 12, 1940. .... $15/12
Buttons, sterling silver with pierced hearts and engraved leaves, English, 1910,
set of six. $150/6
Candy box, cardboard, heart shape, embossed paper, red satin bow. $25
Candy box, heart-shaped cardboard, lithographed, hearts and cherubs. $12
Candy box, red satin, heart shape, gold lace decoration, doves in center. . $35
Candy box, satin covered, Schrafft's, 1930, large size. $20
Candy boxes, nest of three, heart-shaped red cardboard with gold surround,
mid-20th century. $35/3
Candy container, heart shape, papier-mâché, early 20th century. $75

Two early 20th-century, heart-shaped, satin-covered candy boxes.

PRIVATE COLLECTION.

Candy container, mailbox, molded cardboard with silver gummed hearts, early 20th century. $125

Card, acrostic poem, watercolor on paper with human figures in surround, 1805, 7 inches × 9 inches. $1,500

Card, airplane, children, and cherubs, tissue fold-out, 1930. .... $75

Card, airplane, lithographed, with children and honeycomb paper decoration, 1930s. $95

Card, all lace, swirled designs with center cartouche, signed. $45

Card, automobile, children, flower festoons, movable wheels, 1930s. $150

Card, automobile, driver, children, floral bouquets, 1930. .... $75

Card, automobile, honeycomb decoration, Cupids and floral festoons, 1935. ....$125

Mid-19th-century English lottery valentine. COURTESY OF NANCY ROSIN.

A 19th-century bank note valentine. COURTESY OF NANCY ROSIN.

Card, beehive, white ground, handpainted flowers and butterflies, 1825. $400
Card, black boy dressed as soldier, mechanical, embossed cardboard, 1930s.
.... $50
Card, black girl holding basket of flowers, heart surround, early 20th century,
Tuck. $35
Card, box of valentine greetings, 1950. .... $15/box
Card, boy and girl on swing, early 20th century. $9
Card, boy and girl, verse, motto, and butterfly, 1930s. $10
Card, boy, chalkboard, hand moves and erases messages, embossed cardboard,
early 20th century. $15
Card, boy on skis, winter scene, valentine verse, movable. $25
Card, boy dressed as aviator and airplane with heart motif, movable, 1930.
.... $35
Card, boy, movable, easel back, heart surround, 1910. .... $10
Card, calling, flowers, hearts, cherubs, Howland, early 19th century. $20
Card, carriage, children, and flowers, three-dimensional tissue fold-out, 1910.
.... $150
Card, cats in basket, heart and flower festoon, die cut, easel back, honeycomb
tissue fold-out, early 20th century, German. $75
Card, cherubs with movable faces and heart festoons, Tuck, 1910. .... $35
Card, child on bicycle, honeycomb tissue fold-out, embossed cardboard, 1930.
.... $25
Card, children ice skating, winter scene, Grace Drayton, easel back, early 20th
century. $25
Card, children seated in front of radio listening to valentine message, German,
1935. .... $75
Card, comic, fireman saving child, caricature, 1920. .... $15
Card, comic, schoolteacher caricature, circa 1900, crudely colored. $15
Card, coronation coach, honeycomb decoration, 1930. .... $110
Card, Cupids and flower swags, tissue fold-out, 1925. .... $35
Card, Cupids in corners, verse, tissue fold-out, die cut, 1920. .... $35
Card, cut work (Schnerenschnitte) people, animals, hearts, fair condition.
.... $3,500

Late 19th-century valentine.

COURTESY OF NANCY ROSIN.

Late 19th-century, three-dimensional paper valentine.

COURTESY OF JOAN AND ALLAN LEHNER.

Late 19th-century decoupage valentine with embossed paper lace border.

COURTESY OF NANCY ROSIN.

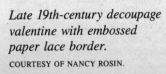

Card, cut work motifs, scalloped embossed border, New England, 1840, 10 inches. $650

Card, Disney dwarf, Sleepy, playing horn, 1938. ....$35

Card, Disney, Snow White, movable figure, 1938. ....$50

Card, double-sided fold-up, watercolor on paper, hearts, flowers, pinwheels, poem, 1800, Pennsylvania, 12½ inches × 12 inches. $3,500

Card, Duke and Duchess of Windsor, applied flower decoration, early 20th century, English. $125

Card, embossed roses and hearts, handwritten verse, circa 1900. ....$35

Card, embossed with pinprick, oval medallion, circa 1850. ....$250

Card, flowers and Cupids with honeycomb fold-out, early 20th century, German. $35

Card, flowers, children, embossed lace paper border, heart in center, late 19th century. $75

Card, fold-out, flowers spell "LOVE," paper lace decoration. $25

Card, fold-out, lace, woman in cartouche, 1940. ....$15

Card, fold-out, silver and white lace surround, handpainted bluebird, signed Meek. $75

Card, fold-out, white lace on flowers, girl's head in heart, 1940. ....$15

Card, fortune teller, tissue paper fold-out, early 20th century. $25

Card, Fraktur, handpainted hearts, geometric motifs and calligraphy, some staining, folded condition, 1820, 6 inches × 8 inches. $1,500

Card, Fraktur, with rebus, handpainted surround, hearts, 1835, fair condition, 12 inches × 14 inches. $2,000

Card, girl and flower festoons, die cut and pierced, circa 1900. ....$35

Card, girl on roller skates, movable, embossed cardboard, 1930. ....$15

Card, girl, pop-up, birds, flowers, hearts, easel back, Tuck. $35

Card, handpainted hearts, ribbons, 19th century, insert with lock of hair. $750

Card, handpainted red hearts, pen and ink verse, late 19th century, American. $450

Card, heart-shaped with lace surround, homemade, early 20th century, large size. $15

Card, honeycomb heart, fold-out, carriage, circa 1920. ....$50

Card, hot air balloon, children, flowers, 1920. ....$50

Card, lace, applied flowers, signed, Feb. 14, 1837. ....$100

Card, lilies, leafage, and hearts, signed, dated 1855. ....$50

Card, locomotive, movable wheels, cherubs, early 20th century. $125

Card, medallion cartouche, embossed, handwritten verse, Meek, 1860, fair condition. $65

Card, ocean liner, children, flowers, honeycomb tissue fold-out, 1930s. ..$135

Card, penny dreadful, doctor caricature. $10

Card, pinpricked with heart, handpainted watercolor surround, fair condition, 4 inches × 6 inches. $750

Card, pink fold-out, silver and lace surround, 1920s. $15

Card, Pinocchio and Jiminy Cricket, movable, 1939. ....$35

Card, Popeye and Olive Oyl, 1943. ....$25

Card, Punch and Judy, heart surround, movable, English, circa 1900. .....$35

Card, rocking horse, boy and girl with hearts, mid-20th century. $3

Card, sachet center, lovers encircled with heart, cameo, lace, signed. $50

Card, sachet, padded, lace border, floral motifs, verse. $45

Card, satin sachet center, gold and white cameo, lace surround, doves at corners, 1930. ....$35

Group of early 20th-century lithographed paper valentines with honeycomb tissue inserts. COURTESY OF NANCY ROSIN.

Card, ship with flowers and hearts outlining portholes, 1930. .... $45
Card, ship, children at portholes, glitter decoration, 1930. .... $125
Card, ship, sailing, honeycomb tissue paper fold-out, 1920, German. $95
Card, suffragette holding placard with heart, early 20th century. $50
Card, train filled with flowers and hearts, pop-up center, circa 1920. ...... $50
Card, train, overflowering floral bouquets, three-dimensional, easel back, 1930s.
.... $150
Card, vinegar valentine, spinster, circa 1870, color lithographed. $10
Card, Wheel of Fortune, movable, early 20th century, with original envelope.
.... $35

Group of late 19th-century valentine catalogs. COURTESY OF NANCY ROSIN.

Card, Wheel of Love, tissue paper fold-out. $14

Card, white cameo lace, handpainted, Howland, mid-19th century. $50

Card, white lace, little girl in center, puzzle verse, signed Whitney. $35

Card, woman wearing pink hat with flowers, parchment paper, early 20th century. $45

Card, wreath, roses, and ferns printed and handpainted, Howland, mid-19th century, fair condition. $75

Carpet beater, wire heart motifs, wooden handle, early 20th century. $125

Centerpiece, cherub holding quiver of arrows, composition with foil-covered cardboard arrows, early 20th century. $50

Centerpiece, cherub, honeycomb tissue fold-out on cardboard base. $25

Centerpiece, heart, red honeycomb tissue paper, cardboard base, mid-20th century. $20

Compact, heart shape, enamel over sterling, English, 1920, with tango chain. $350

Compact, heart shape, painted metal, mid-20th century. $25

Cookie cutter, heart shape, plastic, mid-20th century. $3

Cookie cutter, heart shape, tin, circa 1900. .... $15

Cookie cutters, heart shape, set of three, tin, early 20th century. $35/set

Cups, paper, printed cherubs and ribbon swags, red and white, package. ...$5

Dance card, heart shape, silverplate, celluloid pages, original pencil, early 20th century. $75

Dance card, hearts, paper, souvenir fraternity Valentine's Ball, Sigma Alpha Epsilon, 1952. .... $10

Decoration, garland, embossed foil hearts, mid-20th century. $10

Die cuts, cherubs and flowers, packaged, early 20th century. $35

Die cuts, embossed paper lace trims, package, circa 1910. .... $35

Dish, relish, pressed glass, heart shape, heart and thumbprint pattern, loop handle. $25

Doilies, package, red heart shape, 1940. ....$5

Frame, heart shape, brass, miniature size, 1940. .... $25

Frame, heart shape, double, sterling silver, American, 1920. .... $125

Frame, heart shape, sterling silver, embossed florals, velvet ground, English, 1910, 12 inches high. $425

Frame, Tramp Art, circular shape, with all-over carved hearts, red and gold paint. $1,000

Gift box, coated cardboard, lithographed heart motifs, circa 1940. .... $10

Gift box, coated cardboard, printed hearts and cherubs, handkerchief size. .$3

Handkerchief, printed cotton, hearts and ribbons, scalloped border. $5

Handkerchief, printed cotton, hearts, 1940. ....$5

Hat, crepe paper-covered cardboard with applied cut-out foil-covered cherub. $12

Hearts, package, embossed cardboard, mid-20th century. $10

Invitations, package, heart shape, lithographed, children and flowers, 1930. .... $10

Invitations, package, heart silhouette shape, fair condition. $5

Jug, Sunderland Pottery, "Sailor's Farewell." $1,200

Key ring, heart shape, sterling silver, Tiffany, mid-20th century. $35

Mold, aluminum, heart shape, large, 1940. .... $10

Mold, aluminum, heart, "Happy Valentine's Day," 1940. .... $10

Mold, aspic, hearts, aluminum, box, set of 12, mid-20th century. $5

Mold, butter, wooden carved heart, mid-19th century. $150

Mold, chocolate, heart shape, tin, 10¼ inches. $250
Mold, chocolate, multiple hearts, flat, tin, 14 inches × 18 inches. $150
Mold, copper, heart shape, early 20th century, large size. $225
Mold, ice cream, heart motif with letter, pewter, hinged, early 20th century. $20
Mold, ice cream, hearts entwined, "Love," pewter, hinged, early 20th century. $22
Mold, maple sugar, wooden, 24 hearts, early 19th century. $450
Mold, pudding, copper, tiered heart form, early 20th century. $250
Mold, pudding, ironstone with heart motifs, 1920. ....$35
Napkin ring, silverplate, early 20th century, ring with flower and heart at base. $50
Napkin ring, sterling silver, band with heart center. $35
Napkins, printed heart border, original packaging, circa 1940, Dennison. ...$5
Nut cup, cherub, red crepe paper, water stained, cut-out cardboard. $3
Nut cup, red and white crepe paper, fringed with foil-covered heart and name tag, 1930. ....$5
Nut cup, red crepe paper, name tag and white heart, 1940. ....$5
Pan, cake, heart shape, tin, late 19th century. $75
Paper, waxed, heart motifs, boxed roll, 1940s. $15
Pencil, mechanical, sterling silver with extruded heart, early 20th century, English. $125
Pillow, heart-shaped satin, printed "Happy Valentine's Day." $75
Pin, 14 karat gold, double heart with arrow. $125
Pin, plastic, mid-20th century, entwined hearts. $10
Pin cushion, heart shape, red velvet with shell surround, mid-20th century. $75
Pin cushion, heart shape, sterling surround, Kirk, 1930s. $125
Pin cushion, heart shape, sterling surround, Tiffany. $150

Western Union valentine. COURTESY OF NANCY ROSIN.

Two early 20th-century valentines with children. COURTESY OF JOAN AND
ALLAN LEHNER.

Place card, handpainted Kewpie holding heart with name tag, 1930. .... $10
Place card holders, mirrored glass, handpainted with hearts, set of 12, original box. $35/set
Plaque, heart shape, ceramic, Kewpies in center, signed Rose O'Neill. ...$275
Plaque, Sunderland Luster, "Sailor's Farewell." $325
Plate, Royal Doulton, Valentine, 1976. .... $15
Plate, Royal Doulton, Valentine, 1977. .... $10
Posey holder, filigree, sterling silver, heart-shaped cartouche with engraved monogram, mid-19th century, French. $750
Postcard, arrows through heart, Cupid and flowers, early 20th century. ... $10
Postcard, boy teasing crying girl, hearts and flower swags, early 20th century. $10
Postcard, child dressed in Western Union costume, embossed, early 20th century. $35
Postcard, children dressed as clowns, hearts on costumes. $10
Postcard, Dutch children kissing, Frances Brundage, early 20th century. .. $25
Postcard, Kewpies holding hearts, early 20th century. $35
Postcard, love's message, heart surround with girl wearing bonnet with flowers. $10
Postcard, mailman with valentines, hold-to-light window, early 20th century. $35
Postcard, Palmer Cox Brownie delivering valentines, circa 1910. .... $35
Postcard, winged cherubs, ribbon and verse, early 20th century. $7
Postcard, young woman with flowers, embossed paper lace surround and satin ribbon. $10
Post office box, homemade, crepe paper with gummed stickers, circa 1940. .... $25
Sailor's valentine, shell work and verse, double size, wood surround, English, mid-19th century. $1,000
Scarf, heart motifs, block printed, early 19th century, fair condition. $975
Scrimshaw, busk, floral motifs with color, mid-19th century. $950
Scrimshaw, busk, heart motifs, mid-19th century, fair condition. $1,000
Sheet music, "My Funny Valentine," creased condition. $3
Spoon, caddy, applied heart on handle, sterling silver, American, early 20th century. $125
Spoon, sterling silver, circa 1900, Cupid and quiver. $25
Spoon, sterling silver, early 20th century, heart with arrow. $22
Stickers, package, assorted shapes, hearts, cherubs, flowers, 1930. .... $15

Streamers, crepe paper, printed "Happy Valentine's Day," fair condition. $10

Tablecloth, stenciled paper, hearts, ribbon swags, cherubs, 1920. .... $25

Textile, apron, half, white organdy with applied red hearts, early 20th century. $10

Textile, boxer shorts, cotton, printed hearts, mid-20th century. $5

Textile, hooked rug, "Let Love Be Your Guide," mid-20th century, fine condition, rare. $9,500

Textile, hooked rug, heart motif, late 19th century, faded condition, small size. $450

Textile, penny rug, felt with embroidered edges, multiple heart motifs, early 19th century. $1,500

Textile, table mat, heart motifs, multicolored, embroidered on felt, mid-19th century, 24 inches × 12 inches. $750

Textile, tie, handpainted cherub with heart, silk, 1930. .... $35

Toy, spinning top, wooden with lithographed paper hearts, early 20th century, 3-inch diameter. $25

Traveling ink, heart shape, leather covered, late 19th century. $375

Tray, lithographed tin, Kewpies and hearts, early 20th century. $150

Trivet, heart design, wrought iron with six cut-out hearts, mid-20th century. $45

Trivet, heart shape, brass, cut-out central heart, turned wooden handle, late 19th century. $250

Waffle iron, heart imprints, Griswold Iron, early 20th century. $150

Wall decoration, cardboard, flat embossed cherub with quiver. $15

Wall decoration, doves, embossed cardboard, flower surround. $15

Wall decoration, flat embossed cardboard, heart with floral festoon. $10

Watch chain, sterling silver, Dutch, early 19th century, with applied hearts on filigree fob, key and strap. $425

Watch holder, heart shape, sterling silver, Kirk. $125

The Patriots:
George Washington and
Abraham Lincoln

George Washington, our first president, was known as the Father of Our Country and the Father of Freedom. He remains without question the greatest and most well known of all Americans and he has inspired much devotion. Observance of his birthday, prior to the consolidation of Washington's and Lincoln's birthdays and the establishment of President's Day, used to be on February 22.

February 12 was the date for celebrating Abraham Lincoln's birthday. That date has been replaced by the national observance of President's Day. Red, white, and blue bunting and flags are the best known decorations for commemorating this holiday.

At the time of Washington's death (1799), it was fashionable in the United States to enter into long periods of mourning. During this time, when one attended a funeral, it was customary to receive a commemorative token such as a fob, a locket, a watch paper or something tangible with a memorable reference of the deceased to take home. In their needlework, women created memorial portraits of George Washington depicted in silk and satin. For the greater part of the 100 years following Washington's death, it was not unusual to celebrate the man and his life (but not with the party atmosphere we usually associate with a celebration). The centennial (1876) of our country's founding increased the fervor with which Washington was revered and, by that time, postcards and commemorative fabric handkerchiefs were printed with his likeness.

Sterling silver spoons with medallion heads depicting George Washington were introduced in the late nineteenth century. These were followed by spoons commemorating the inauguration of Washington. Another spoon was manufactured with a portrait of our first president as portrayed in Gilbert Stuart's painting. This was surmounted by an eagle with a cherry tree on the reverse.

The legend of George's honesty about his truthfulness when queried if he did indeed chop down his father's cherry tree inspired the creation of many holiday ornaments. Early 20th-century German- and American-made pressed board hatchets, cherry trees, and stumps with clusters of cherries alone and alongside the stumps are available. Cardboard logs with pictures of Washington and full-figure papier-mâché busts of Washington alone can be found. Many of these items are candy containers with removable parts.

Washington's Birthday Listings

Advertising, paper label, General Washington on white horse, 1940, good condition. $10
Bank, figure of Washington, cast iron, early 20th century, 6¼ inches high. $95
Bookends, George Washington, painted cast iron, early 20th century. ...$40/pr
Bottle, liquor Jacquin, cobalt blue glass bust of Washington, miniature size. $12
Bread plate, pressed glass, "George Washington: Father of Our Country," late 19th century. $50
Candles, pair, George and Martha Washington figures, 1940s. $25/pr
Candy container, cardboard log, George Washington's face, lithographed paper, early 20th century. $100
Candy container, George Washington lifts off circular stand holding an American flag, multicolored, 4 inches high. $75
Candy container, George Washington riding horse, bisque head, composition body, early 20th century, German. $1,000
Candy container, George Washington, early 20th century, German, bisque head, figure on dapple gray horse, felt outfit, felt-covered horse with glass eyes, very fine condition, 11 inches high. $1,200
Candy container, hatchet, red, white, and blue crepe-covered cardboard, 1930s. $55
Candy container, log with applied cherries, cardboard, early 20th century. $75
Candy container, log, cardboard with hatchet and cherries, 1930s. $60
Candy container, Washington, bust, papier-mâché, early 20th century. ... $110

Early 20th-century candy containers: left, *hatchet;* right, *log with Washington's head.* COURTESY OF PAM AND CHRIS RUSSELL.

*Early 20th-century
candles in the form of
George and Martha
Washington, $25/pr.*

Cookie cutter, hatchet, tin, early 20th century, large size. $75
Doorstop, George Washington, cast iron, early 20th century. $550
Lithograph, "Death of Washington," Currier and Ives, framed, 13 inches × 17
inches. $35
Lithograph, "General George Washington," Currier and Ives, framed, 14 inches
× 10 inches. $55
Mold, ice cream, George Washington bust, pewter hinged, early 20th century.
.... $65
Mold, ice cream, hinged log, pewter, early 20th century. $45
Mold, ice cream, Washington chopping cherry tree, iron, early 20th century.
.... $75
Mold, ice cream, Washington on horse, pewter hinge, early 20th century. . $65
Nut basket, woven, with applied cherries and cellophane grass in center, early
20th century. $22
Nut cup, crepe paper with cardboard cherry decoration. $5
Nut cup, double-frill crepe paper with composition cherries, 1940. .... $10
Plate, "Life of Washington," ceramic, 9-inch diameter. $25
Spoon, sterling silver, figure of George Washington, early 20th century. ... $18
Trivet, George Washington, cast and pierced iron, early 20th century. $35

Lincoln's Birthday Listings

Advertising, candy container, Log Cabin Syrup, lithographed tin, early 20th
century. $350
Bank, Abraham Lincoln, glass bottle, tin closure. $25
Bookends, Abraham Lincoln sitting on bench, bronze patina on plaster, early
20th century. $35/pr
Bookends, Abraham Lincoln standing by chair, bronzed metal, early 20th cen-
tury. $35/pr
Bottle, Lincoln figure, clear glass, converts to bank, mid-20th century. $10
Plate, Abraham Lincoln, Wedgwood, blue jasperware, mid-20th century. . $95

Saint Patrick's Day

It is not known when or how the celebration of this holiday began other than as an occasion for the Irish to pay tribute to their homeland. Saint Patrick was the first Irish saint to use the shamrock as a symbol of the Trinity. Legend says that he is the person responsible for driving the snakes from Ireland. March 17, chosen as his day to be both a holiday and a holy day, was first celebrated in the United States in Boston in 1737. Ireland celebrates the day as a religious holiday. In the United States, however, the celebration encompasses parades, parties, the wearing of the green, and the drinking of green beer, even if one is not Irish.

Leprechauns (the little people of Ireland), four-leaf clovers, fairies, pots of gold, and the Blarney Stone are the symbols for the holiday. These are seen in early 20th-century pressed cardboard candy containers made in Germany and America. Other symbols depict Paddy the Irishman with his pigs, Irish boy and girl dancers, pipe candy containers, and green top hats. Banners stating "Erin Go Bragh" ("Ireland Forever"), party favors, and paper table decorations with green shamrocks can be found.

Saint Patrick's Day Listings

Banner, cloth, stenciled "Erin Go Bragh," 1930s. $75
Candy container, bottle, full-figure Irish Whiskey covered with green crinkle paper and paper label. $65
Candy container, bust of Irishman, handpainted molded cardboard, opens on bottom. $75
Candy container, clay pipe, cardboard covered with crinkled green paper and a shamrock with white ribbon near tip. $125
Candy container, head of Irishman with pipe, papier-mâché, painted. $225
Candy container, Irish boy and girl couple standing on cardboard candy box, German, early 20th century. $325
Candy container, Irish gentleman, on papier-mâché base, German, early 20th century. $250
Candy container, Irish lass, papier-mâché, on green and white cardboard box, early 20th century. $75
Candy container, Irishman with top hat and shillelagh on wood base, head is removable, 8 inches high, German, 1930. .... $250

Candy container, pig, large, with shamrock in mouth, papier-mâché, early 20th century. $150

Candy container, pig, with top hat and shamrock, molded paper-mâché with whistle at back, German, early 20th century. $450

Candy container, top hat, cardboard with crinkled green paper with attached wire four-leaf clover. $100

Candy container, top hat, shamrock in hat band, green and white cardboard, early 20th century. $75

Centerpiece, top hat, honeycomb tissue paper fold-out with cardboard base and shamrock at band, 1940. .... $35

Cup and saucer, glazed pottery, Happy St. Patrick's Day, early 20th century. $15

Cups, paper, green and white shamrocks, original cellophane package. $5

Favor, pipe, clay, circa 1920. .... $10

Garland, honeycomb tissue paper fold-out, green and white, 12 inches, mid-20th century. $15

Handkerchief, linen, embroidered shamrock, handcrocheted green border. .$5

Handkerchief, printed cotton, border of shamrocks, 1940. ....$5

Invitations, shamrocks and leprechauns, printed paper, package, 1940. ......$5

Nut cup, crepe paper, cardboard cut-out Paddy and pig. $10

Nut cup, double-frill green and white crepe paper with cardboard shamrock. $5

Party hat, top hat, foil-covered cardboard with shamrock. $20

Place card, leprechaun with pot of gold and name tag. $5

Place cards, four-leaf clovers, three with original name tags. $5/3

Postcard, boy and girl dancing Irish jig, shamrocks with ribbons, embossed cardboard, early 20th century. $10

Sheet music, "Danny Boy," fair condition, 1940s. $5

Sheet music, "When Irish Eyes Are Smiling," 1930s. $10

Streamers, crepe paper, green and white stripes, package. $5

Tablecloth, Irish linen, embroidered shamrocks, early 20th century. $75

Tablecloth, printed paper, leprechauns, shamrocks in green and white, original cellophane package, mid-20th century. $10

Wall decoration, group of four shamrocks, pressed cardboard cut-out, 1940. ....$15/4

Wall decoration, Irish harp, embossed "Erin Go Bragh," cardboard. $10

Pair of early 20th-century candy containers in the form of Irish lass and gentleman.
COURTESY OF PAM AND CHRIS RUSSELL.

Purim

Purim is an early spring festival celebrated by the Jews, usually in March, to commemorate the Biblical story of Esther. When Haman, one of the court ministers, wanted to destroy the Persian Jews, Esther interceded for the Jews with King Ahasuerus. Purim means "lots" because the day chosen to exterminate the Jews was determined by the casting of lots.

Today the scroll or megillat (story) of Esther is read in the synagogue. The scroll rolls into a tube or case to protect the parchment or leather upon which it is written when it is not being used. Cases were made in sterling silver, wood or ivory, sometimes decorated with garnets or turquoise stones. Cases and scrolls are very scarce in the marketplace.

Through the years, whenever the story of Esther is read in the synagogue, noisemakers, known as groggers or rattles, are sounded whenever Haman's name is mentioned. Groggers were made of wood, occasionally with a whistle. More affluent families had sterling silver noisemakers decorated with Hebrew inscriptions or Purim motifs. In further cele-

Contemporary sterling silver grogger (noisemaker) for Purim, $1,000; dreidel (top) for Chanukah, $350.

COURTESY OF GRAND STERLING.

bration of the holiday, children also dress up as characters from the story of Esther and take gifts of food to family or friends. Special plates called "Shlach Manot plates," which derives from the book of Esther and means "send portions of food," are used for taking these sweetmeats. Made in pewter or pottery, older styles of these plates are extremely rare, with those in sterling silver even rarer.

Purim Listings

Costume, Queen Esther, purple silk dress with puffed sleeves, white apron, gold cardboard crown, homemade, early 20th century, fair condition. $25

Favor, crown, cardboard, with attached net bag of candy. $5

Grogger (noisemaker), sterling silver, embossed Purim symbols, reproduction. $1,000

Grogger (noisemaker), wooden ratchet type, early 20th century. $35

Mask, King Ahasuerus, netting stiffened with sizing, handpainted with attached beard, early 20th century. $75

Mask, Queen Esther, half-mask, satin with lace frill, 1930. .... $10

Photograph, Sunday-school play, Queen Esther, King Ahasuerus, and Haman, signed on reverse, Brooklyn, 1927. .... $35

Plate, Shlach Manot, ceramic, transfer printed symbols, handpainted border, 12-inch diameter. $325

Plate, Shlach Manot, pewter, embossed Purim symbols, late 19th century, Continental. $1,200

Scroll, Esther, Persian, wooden, boxed, illuminated, the box painted with images of Haman on the gallows, victorious Mordecai and appropriate Hebrew inscriptions around; vellum scroll with floral garlands between columns, manuscript in Hebrew in square script—"Hamelech" scroll. $3,500

Easter

Easter, one of the holiest days of the Christian calendar, commemorates the rising of Christ from the dead to eternal life. This religious celebration in the spring of the year has also evolved into an observance and adoration of new life, especially related to flowers and flowering plants. The word Easter is derived from *oestera* or *ostre*, indicating the relationship between a joyous Christian festival and pagan celebrations in honor of the Anglo-Saxon goddess of spring.

It was probably at some point during the eighteenth century that coloring and decorating eggs at Easter became a favored ritual because, since the beginning of time, eggs have been symbols of eternal life. From this custom the use of papier-mâché and cardboard eggs evolved, many with handpainted and gaily decorated designs. Traditional Slavic eggs, made from real eggs with the insides blown out, were hand-decorated and given as gifts or exchanged as tokens of love or friendship. Other cultures made eggs completely from sugar and decorated them with flower

Group of late 19th-, early and mid-20th-century Easter eggs in various forms. COURTESY OF BARB AND DICK SHILVOCK.

motifs, often with a window exposing an intricately designed family or other genre scene, sometimes with animals. The rolling of Easter eggs on a field or lawn symbolized the rolling of the stone away from the tomb of Christ. Today this celebration continues to be an annual event at the White House.

Additional favored symbols for the holiday are the Easter lily, commemorating the resurrection of Christ. Newly born animals, such as bunny rabbits, baby chicks, and lambs, are also decorative motifs used for the holiday.

The tradition of the Easter bunny in this country was introduced by the Pennsylvania Germans in the early eighteenth century. Children, believing that at the beginning of springtime the Easter bunny would bring eggs to hide in the grass, would leave their bonnets on their doorsteps at night hoping for the Easter rabbit to fill them with colored eggs. From this evolved the custom of filling baskets with eggs, paper, candies, and cellophane grass. Even today, children leave containers, usually baskets, to be filled by the bunny with foil-wrapped candy eggs as well as colored ones and multicolored jelly beans.

During the latter part of the nineteenth century in New England, sterling silver spoons to commemorate Easter were manufactured. Some had handles which depicted the Easter lily with a cross. Others were decorated with a chick hatching from an egg, and yet others had an engraved scene in the bowl depicting Christ rising from the tomb.

When Irving Berlin wrote his well-known song "Easter Parade" in the early 1900s, he did not create the idea for the famous procession on

Early 20th-century velvet Easter rabbit with carrot, $595. COURTESY OF TERRY AND JOE DZIADUL.

Group of early 20th-century full-figure rabbit candy containers.
COURTESY OF JOAN AND ALLAN LEHNER.

New York City's Fifth Avenue. Easter parades, with the participants donning new clothing and wearing special Easter bonnets or hats, evolved from Roman times during the reign of Constantine and signified a new beginning, again the revival of the life cycles in the spring of the year.

At the turn of the twentieth century, cardboard candy containers from Germany were introduced in the form of rabbits, chickens, ducks, and eggs. Many of these had removable fabric clothing and blown glass eyes. Other popular containers were inspired by the Palmer Cox Brownies, Rose O'Neill Kewpies, Campbell Kids, and even Foxy Grandpa. Many of these were also used as toys because they were able to be placed upon horses, goats, wagons, and, later, cars. Some were produced with wind-up mechanisms for walking and others enclosed music boxes. Often made with removable tops or bases, homemade or store-bought sweets filled the figures. Materials such as cotton batting simulated fur and, occasionally, real chicken feathers were used as wings. Candy containers continued to be made in America, Germany, and Japan through the middle part of the twentieth century. Some of the early twentieth-century German candy containers were available for purchase in New York City at the famous toy store F.A.O. Schwarz.

Brightly colored painted and lithographed tin egg-shaped candy containers became popular in the 1930s. These were followed by cardboard examples and molded clear glass containers. Several are found in the form of full-figure rabbits, including one holding a carrot.

In the early part of the twentieth century, party tables were decorated with full-figure cardboard chicks and rabbits. Individual nut cups were in the form of woven paper and crepe paper-covered baskets. Party table colors were usually lavender, yellow, and white with printed floral motifs. Grass and floral-strewn motifs were common for table covers while those for children's parties were decorated with rabbits, chickens, and brightly colored Easter eggs. Baskets, baby chicks or rabbits made of crepe paper over wire bases were often table centerpieces. Sometimes one of the animals would be portrayed riding in a moss-covered cardboard cart. Matching printed napkins, tablecloths, plates, cups, and invitations could be purchased at the local party store.

Hollow and solid chocolate rabbits and bunnies, ranging in sizes from 2 inches to 3 feet, decorated tables and mantelpieces, and were also given as gifts. Made in full figure, the original tin and pewter molds by Schrafft's and other chocolate makers are on the market today. Figural ice cream molds and cookie cutters depicting the Easter lily, rabbits, and chicks in various sizes were also popular. During the early part of the twentieth century, costumes were part of the Easter celebration. Most popular was the Easter bunny, both in homemade and store-bought versions.

Punched or perforated paper mottoes, also known as Berlin work and made at the turn of the twentieth century, proclaimed greetings for the holiday. Some merely stated "Happy Easter"; others depicted the cross and the motto "Simply to Thy Cross I Cling."

A common practice dating from the early part of the twentieth century included sending postal and greeting cards for the holiday. Among these, which are now extremely collectible, are examples displaying Palmer Cox Brownies, Easter rabbits with baskets of eggs, Kewpies, Easter lilies, churches, and Easter eggs.

Easter Listings

Advertising, store display, cardboard, Easter bunny holding colored food dyes. $25
Advertising, tin, cookies, Easter greetings. $10
Banner, homemade cotton, "Happy Easter," with chicks and bunnies embroidery, 1930s, doorway size, fair condition, stained. $45
Basket, cardboard, woven, cellophane grass, cotton batting chicks. $25
Basket, chenille, miniature, with chenille chicks, early 20th century. $55
Basket, child's, woven paper with grass and candy eggs, 1940. .... $35
Basket, cookie, lithographed print rabbits and chicks, sewn sides, 1930. .. $25
Basket, "Easter Greetings," printed lithographed paper, sewn sections, early 20th century. $30
Basket, twig, with grass and chenille chicks, early 20th century, American. $75
Baskets, four, including one large, one small, twig variety, excellent condition. $5/all
Baskets, group of five, various sizes. $10/5
Baskets, group of four, woven, various sizes and colors, most 3 inches to 5 inches. $5/4
Book, Peter Cottontail, 1940. .... $10
Books, paper, group of children's stories with rabbits and chickens, small size, some damage to covers. $10/lot

Bunnies and chicks, three, Germany and Japan, circa 1930s, polychromed, the bunnies on haunches, two with glass eyes, damaged, 4 inches to 9 inches high. $150/3

Candy box, lithographed cardboard, chicks and bunnies with ribbons at neck, poor condition. $8

Candy box, lithographed cardboard, square, bunnies and carrots, mid-20th century. $10

Candy boxes, lot, three, printed paper, Easter motifs, some damage. $8/3

Candy container, bunny, egg, papier-mâché, 4½ inches. $75

Candy container, chick emerging from egg, Germany, papier-mâché, circa 1910. .... $75

Candy container, chick, circa 1920, glass eyes. $150

Candy container, chick, egg, pressed paper, glass eyes, ribbon, 5½ inches. $80

Candy container, chick, glass eyes, wire spring feet, circa 1930. .... $175

Candy container, chick, in eggshell automobile, replaced closure. $325

Candy container, chick, standing, original paint and closure, candy, 2¼ inches. $125

Candy container, chicken on nest, 1930s. $75

Candy container, duck, 1920s. $75

Candy container, duck, composition, 1920s. $125

Candy container, duck, walking, papier-mâché, early 20th century, wearing peasant costume. $750

Candy container, egg shape, flower, lithographed paper, German, circa 1940. .... $20

Candy container, egg shape, lithographed tin, 1930. .... $50

Candy container, egg, papier-mâché, circa 1930. .... $75

Candy container, egg, papier-mâché, mid-20th century. $25

Candy container, egg, rabbit, lithographed paper, German, mid-20th century. $25

Candy container, Foxy Grandpa on rabbit, early 20th century. $475

Candy container, hen on Easter egg, lithographed tin, early 20th century. $50

Early 20th-century Easter rabbit candy container with papier-mâché and lithographed cardboard eggs.
COURTESY OF JOAN AND ALLAN LEHNER.

Candy container, rabbit driving car, early 20th century. $500

Candy container, rabbit eating carrot, circa 1940, 4³⁄₈ inches. $50

Candy container, rabbit eating carrot, glass, clear, 4¹⁄₂ inches. $50

Candy container, rabbit in basket, glass eyes, papier-mâché, 10¹⁄₂ inches. $125

Candy container, rabbit on all fours, papier-mâché, 1940. .... $50

Candy container, rabbit playing golf, papier-mâché, Germany, early 20th century. $450

Candy container, rabbit pulling cart, wooden, Germany, 8 inches. $225

Candy container, rabbit pulling wood and tin cart, German. $250

Candy container, rabbit sitting up, pressed glass. $25

Candy container, rabbit standing with basket at back, pressed paper, glass eyes, uncolored. $35

Candy container, rabbit standing with basket at side, pressed paper, early 20th century, uncolored. $25

Candy container, rabbit, basket on arm, papier-mâché, 5 inches. $125

Candy container, rabbit, basket on back, cloth covered, circa 1920. ......$150

Candy container, rabbit, early 1900s, papier-mâché, pulling moss cart. ..$450

Candy container, rabbit, early 20th century, Germany, papier-mâché, sitting-up brown bunny, glass eyes (two legs repaired), height 16 inches. $250

Candy container, rabbit, early 20th century, Germany, papier-mâché, standing brown rabbit with carrot in mouth, glass eyes (left rear leg repaired), 10¹⁄₂ inches × 11¹⁄₄ inches. $275

Candy container, rabbit, fur covered, composition, carrot in mouth, circa 1900, 6 inches. $225

Candy container, rabbit, fur covered, Germany, 1910–20, 9 inches. $250

Candy container, rabbit, laid-back ears, glass, clear. $55

Candy container, rabbit, nodder, 10¹⁄₂ inches. $600

Candy container, rabbit, nodder, papier-mâché, early 20th century. $325

Candy container, rabbit, papier-mâché, 9 inches. $125

Candy container, rabbit, papier-mâché, early 20th century, German, head separates, dressed in apron. $475

Candy container, rabbit, papier-mâché, Germany, 7 inches. $100

Candy container, rabbit, papier-mâché, glass eyes, brown, 8¹⁄₂ inches. $200

Candy container, rabbit, pressed cardboard, 8 inches. $75

Candy container, rabbit, pulling cart, early 20th century. $275

Candy container, rabbit, pushing chick in wheelbarrow, papier-mâché. . $500

Candy container, rabbit, removable head, pressed cardboard, 5¹⁄₂ inches. $125

Candy container, rabbit, seated, 1920. ....$125

Candy container, rabbit, seated, glass, 6¹⁄₄ inches. $35

Candy container, rabbit, twig cart, papier-mâché, brown. $325

Candy container, rooster, papier-mâché, early 20th century. $150

Candy containers, bunny rabbit, four, early 20th century, German, papier-mâché, three with glass eyes, two sitting up, one standing (slight damage), height 4 inches × 6 inches. $375/lot

Candy containers, egg, two, one with rabbit and chicken, the other with Dutch children on side, early 20th century. $125/2

Candy containers, rabbits, pair, dressed as boy and girl, early 20th century, German, good condition, height 10 inches. $500/pr

Centerpiece, egg, honeycomb tissue paper on cardboard base, 1940. ....$25

Group of early 20th-century Easter candy containers. COURTESY OF JOAN
AND ALLAN LEHNER.

Centerpiece, table, bunny rabbit, cardboard with honeycomb tissue paper fold-
out on cardboard base, 1940. .... $35
Centerpiece, table, honeycomb tissue, duck with cardboard web feet. $35
Centerpiece, woven paper basket filled with small honeycomb tissue Easter eggs,
early 20th century. $35
Chickens, six, early 20th century, papier-mâché, several are candy containers
(some paint loss and damage). $125/6
Cookie cutter, Easter lily, with backplate, tin, late 19th century. $18
Cookie cutter, egg shape, tin, late 19th century. $5
Cookie cutter, rabbit, upright position, tin, early 20th century. $15
Costume, Easter bunny, homemade with felt ears, mid-20th century, child size.
.... $15
Doorstop, Peter Rabbit, cast iron, painted decoration, early 20th century.
....$425
Egg, bunnies eating carrots, printed tin, mid-20th century. $25
Egg, celluloid, with hen and chicks, weighted bottom. $30
Egg, ceramic, pink marbled and gold stripe together with early decorated egg,
hold-to-light and view of bird inside, mid-20th century. $30/2
Egg, green, cardboard and chromolithographed, fine condition, 1940. ...... $35

*Early 20th-century duck table centerpiece,
cardboard and honeycomb tissue paper.*
COURTESY OF JOAN AND ALLAN LEHNER.

Group of early and mid-20th-century lithographed paper Easter eggs. COURTESY OF JOAN AND ALLAN LEHNER.

Egg, lot of two, cardboard and chromolithographed, fine condition, 1940. ....$65/2

Egg, milk glass, blown, flat bottom, chick design, handpainted, circa 1900. .... $35

Egg, milk glass, "Easter Greetings," 6 inches. $50

Egg, milk glass, embossed chick, early 20th century, 2½ inches. $30

Egg, molded cardboard, frosted decoration, view in end, early 20th century, good condition. $50

Egg, scenes of egg rolling, lithographed tin, opens as candy container, 1940. .... $35

Egg containers, chromolithographed, two, one with duck, rabbits, and chicks, the other two children and chicks, mid-20th century. $65/2

Egg cup, glazed pottery, Easter egg. $35

Figure, nodder, rabbit dressed as little boy, papier-mâché, 5 inches high. $275

Figure, nodder, rabbit dressed as little girl, papier-mâché, poor condition, 6 inches high, Germany. $75

Figures, bunny, eight, early 20th century, papier-mâché, in various poses, six are candy containers, six have glass eyes (some lot damage and repairs). $75/8

Figures, bunny, seven and a farmer, early 20th century, papier-mâché, two bunnies and a farmer on a corn shock candy container, three assorted bunnies and one bunny pulling a cart, velveteen bunny with glass eyes (slight damage to lot). $175/all

Figures, bunny, six, 20th century, three papier-mâché, three plaster of Paris, five are candy containers (some lot wear), height 6 inches to 7½ inches. $200/6

Figures, bunny, 20, 20th century, in various poses and sizes, papier-mâché: nine candy containers, five sitting; five plaster of Paris; one plastic with glass eyes (some lot damage). $125/all

Figures, ducks, four, 20th century, papier-mâché, three wearing outfits, one opens bill when body is pressed down, all in good condition, height 5 inches to 7 inches. $150/4

Game, bowling, papier-mâché rabbits, late 19th century. $1,500

Gift box, pressed cardboard, lithographed with bunnies and eggs, mid-20th century, shirt-box size. $5

Invitations, basket of eggs, package. $5

Invitations, bunnies, "Easter Greetings," package. $5

Menu, Easter dinner, handpainted, homemade, 1897. .... $20

Mold, aspic, reclining rabbit, pressed glass, 1940. .... $45

Mold, cake, lamb, Griswold with booklet and recipes. $75

Mold, cake, with sitting rabbit, iron. $150

Mold, chocolate, rabbit in Easter egg, tin, early 20th century. $75

Mold, chocolate, rabbit pulling Easter egg cart, tin, early 20th century. $65

Mold, chocolate, rabbit with floppy ears eating carrot, circa 1900. ....$100

Mold, chocolate, rabbits, four, early 20th century, tin, Germany. $85

Mold, chocolate, rabbits, standing, tin, early 20th century, 13 inches high. $125

Mold, cookie, springerle, wooden, hen on nest, early 20th century. $125

Mold, cookie, springerle, wooden, rabbits, early 20th century. $135

Mold, cookie, springerle, wooden, rabbits, reproduction. $75

Mold, ice cream, Easter lily, pewter, early 20th century. $50

Mold, ice cream, lily, iron, early 20th century. $45

Napkin ring, figural, chick on wishbone, "Best Wishes," Derby, silverplate, early 20th century. $75

Napkin ring, figurine, chick on wishbone, "Best Wishes," Derby, silverplate, fair condition. $45

Napkins, printed paper, bunny in children's clothing, circa 1940, original cellophane package. $5

Needlework, motto, punched paper, "Happy Easter." $75

Novelty, egg-dying kit, original package. $5

Nut cup, basket shape, crepe paper-covered cardboard with cut-out chick emerging from egg, 1930. .... $10

Nut cup, crepe paper, purple and white, cardboard Easter lily cut-out and name tag. $3

Nut cup, yellow crepe paper, name tag and cardboard rabbit cut-out, 1940. ....$5

Place card, figure, peanut dressed as chick. $10

Place cards, duck, full figure, cardboard on base with name tag. $10

Plate, Frankoma Pottery, 1972. .... $20

Postcard, boy and girl carrying flowers, embossed "Easter Greetings," early 20th century. $5

Postcard, chick coming out of shell, four chicks and flowers, "Happy Easter." $10

Postcard, chicken emerging from egg, flowers. $5

Postcard, chicken in straw hat next to vegetables. $5

Postcard, girl with dog on leash, Drayton, early 20th century, "Happy Easter." $25

Postcard, hold-to-light, rabbit with chicks, circa 1900. .... $35

Postcard, woman in Victorian costume, plumed hat, early 20th century. $5

Rabbit, sitting, papier-mâché with glass eyes, together with 6-inch-high chick with open eggshell. $75/2

Seals, gummed back, Easter lily, package. $3

Sheet music, "Easter Parade." $10

Spoon, chick hatching from egg, sterling silver. $20

Spoon, sterling silver, Easter lily. $18

Tablecloth, printed cotton, flowers and rabbits. $25

Tablecloth, printed paper, Easter lilies and ribbon swags. $10

Tablecloth, printed paper, rabbits, chicks, and eggs. $10

Table decoration, chicken on a nest, molded cardboard, lifts off to reveal candy eggs inside, 1940. ....$100

Table decoration, rabbit, composition with painted decoration, 6 inches long. $75

Tin, cookie, oval, lithographed with Easter scenes, swing handles, used as lunch box. $20

Toy, piñata, standing Easter rabbit with carrot, mid-20th century, Mexican, with candies and toys. $35

Toys and decorations, lot, 20th century, candy containers: four German lithographed eggs, one with chicks; pair of standing storks; birds; baskets with cotton chicks; metal, glass, and ceramic eggs; composition bunnies; duck pull-toy (minor wear to lot). $200/all

Wall decoration, basket of eggs with rabbits and glitter, 1930. .... $15

Wall decoration, duck with ducklings, embossed cardboard, cut-out, 1940. .... $10

Wall decoration, "Happy Easter," embossed lithographed cardboard, 1940. ....$5

May Day

May 1, designated as May Day, was established in celebration of Flora, the goddess of flowers, to signal the changing of the seasons. In the late eighteenth and early nineteenth centuries, a young sapling was stripped of its leaves and branches and then wrapped with colorful pastel flowers and ribbons in celebration of "bringing in the May." Village children danced under the May tree or pole with bouquets of flowers. At this time the May Queen, usually the prettiest of the young maidens in the village, was crowned. She was greeted with flowers and hoops decorated with ribbons and bells and crowned with a wreath of fresh flowers, usually daisies. The custom of rolling the hoop continues today at several colleges in the United States.

In the nineteenth century, May baskets filled with fresh flowers, candy, and verse were secretly hung on doors in expressions of friendship and romance. Esther Howland of Massachusetts, well known for producing valentine and other greeting cards, made exquisite May baskets which sold for up to $10 each, an exorbitant sum for the time.

During the early and mid-20th century, table centerpieces made as miniature Maypoles with crepe paper ribbons extended from the centerpiece to each guest's place at the table. Nut cups in the form of May baskets and crowns of field flowers for each guest are still to be found. Although not common, Maypoles are still available.

May Day Listings

Basket, woven paper, bentwood handle, ribbon streamers and wax flowers, 1930. .... $28

Basket, woven straw, ribbon-wrapped handle, crepe paper flowers, 1920. . $25

Centerpiece, Maypole, ribbon-wrapped cardboard, with flowers and ribbon streamers, 1930. .... $125

Centerpiece, woven basket, filled with crepe paper flowers and ribbons, early 20th century. $25

Garland, tissue paper flowers with ribbon bow knots, early 20th century. . $25

Hat, crown, crepe paper daisies on wreath frame, early 20th century. $18

Hat, crown, gold foil covered with embossed flowers, 1940. ....$5

Hat, crown, tissue paper flowers and leaves over wire frame. $15

Invitation, flower basket, handpainted cut-out cardboard, dated May 1. .....$7
Maypole, turned wooden pole with circular wooden supports, late 19th century, probably American, 7 feet tall. $2,500
Maypole, wrought iron pole in the form of open work umbrella, cast iron base, early 20th century, American, 6 feet tall. $1,500
Nut basket, crepe paper-covered cardboard, gummed seal depicting flowers and name tag. $5
Photograph, children dancing around Maypole, English village, early 20th century. $35

Independence Day:
The Fourth of July

Independence Day, declared by the Continental Congress to be a national day for joyous observance and later, by John Adams, as a day for fireworks and other expressions of joy, celebrated the signing of the Declaration of America's Independence from England on July 4, 1776. It is the most secular and patriotic of America's holidays and one of the few saved from the practice of a designated Friday or Monday date to create a three-day weekend.

Since the beginning of the celebration of this holiday, entire towns, villages, and individual families have had parties, picnics, balls, and parades. Bonfires and fireworks often accompanied these gatherings. Band concerts, which began in the early part of the nineteenth century, are still very much a part of this holiday. Patriotic cloth and paper bunting in red, white, and blue were hung on public buildings and homes to mark this day. At nighttime, parade torches, most with patriotic motifs depicting eagles and shields, were used.

Early 20th-century fabric bunting, $350.

The Liberty Bell, cast in England in 1751, arrived in the United States intact but cracked as it was being tested. Probably the most important and one of the most exciting times the bell was rung was on July 8, 1776, to proclaim the adoption of the Declaration of Independence by the United States of America. It is thought that the earliest glass candy container was made in the form of the Liberty Bell for sale during the centennial exhibition in 1876. During the early and through to the middle part of the twentieth century, figural glass candy containers in the form of the Liberty Bell, sometimes filled with red, white, and blue ball candies, were popular.

Other common symbols to commemorate America's special day include Uncle Sam and his hat. Samuel Wilson was a government inspector of supplies for the army in 1812. His supplies were always stamped "U.S." to mean United States which later, through usage, became a symbol for Uncle Sam. Milk glass candy containers in the form of Uncle Sam's hat painted with stars and stripes were made at the time of the centennial as well as full-figure clear glass containers depicting Independence Hall. Brightly colored papier-mâché and cardboard figural candy containers in the form of this famous man were popular from the latter part of the nineteenth until the middle part of the twentieth centuries.

Additional emblems used as figural candy containers for this holiday were Liberty caps, depictions of Miss Liberty, shields, flags, and stars. All, of course, were usually painted in red, white, and blue, some with stars and stripes as decoration. Other cardboard candy containers were produced in the form of top hats and firecrackers with string fuses, always in red, white, and blue, sometimes decorated all over with star motifs. These symbols were most commonly used in the latter part of the nineteenth and the early part of the twentieth centuries on pressed cardboard and paper candy containers made in Germany and America. Some were also produced in molded glass.

Costumes from the early part of the twentieth century almost always included Uncle Sam complete with his top hat and striped trousers. Other costumes depicted Miss Liberty.

Paper party and table favors and decorations used these motifs, again in red, white, and blue. Often they were printed in red and white stripes with blue and white star borders in matching ensembles of tablecloths, plates, napkins, cups, and nut cups. Red, white, and blue bunting decorated the interior and exterior of the house while red, white, and blue crepe paper streamers crisscrossed the room accented with honeycomb tissue paper Liberty Bells. Miniature paper American flags were used for table decorations, on top of frosted cakes or as party favors.

Spoons from the late nineteenth century were manufactured in sterling silver and depicted the Liberty Bell at the handle. Others portrayed Uncle Sam in full figure, some with the Capitol engraved in the bowl.

Chocolate and ice cream molds depicted Stars and Stripes, the Liberty Bell, and the Shield of Liberty. These were first made in the late nineteenth century and continue to be popular today.

Berlin work mottoes were made in a series for the celebration of the centennial. They included sayings and pictures stating: "Long May It Wave," "Stars & Stripes," "1776–1876" with pictures of George Washington and Abraham Lincoln, and "Centennial." To retain their value, these pieces must be in pristine condition in original frames.

Holiday greetings in the form of postal and greeting cards were popular during the early part of the twentieth century. Many portrayed children carrying flags or little boys dressed in soldier or sailor uniforms leading the band of glory. The Liberty Bell was also a popular motif.

Independence Day Listings

Advertising, bank, Liberty Bell, Nash's Mustard, glass, early 20th century. $20
Advertising, pail, Liberty Bell Candy, lithographed tin, early 20th century. $295
Advertising, tray, Liberty Ice Cream, pictures Liberty Bell, papier-mâché and printed paper, early 20th century. $35
Bank, Liberty Bell, carnival glass, 1930. .... $10
Bank, Liberty Bell, cast iron, early 20th century, 4 inches high. $45
Bank, Liberty Bell, Centennial Money Bank, 1876. .... $50
Bank, Liberty Bell, milk glass, metal closure, circa 1910. .... $12
Bank, Liberty Bell, patinated white metal, wood closure, 7 inches high. . $110
Bank, Uncle Sam, mechanical, late 19th century. $1,550

Early 20th-century wooden mechanical toy. COURTESY OF JOAN AND ALLAN LEHNER.

Group of candy containers.
COURTESY OF JOAN AND ALLAN LEHNER.

Bookends, Liberty Bell, bronze patina on pot metal, early 20th century.
....$25/pr
Bottle opener, Uncle Sam, cast iron, painted, early 20th century. $35
Bunting, parade, late 19th century, American eagle in center. $150
Bunting, red, white, and blue crepe paper, cut-out foil-covered star in center,
early 20th century. $35
Candy container, firecracker, cardboard, red, white, and blue with string fuse,
embossed "Happy 4th," early 20th century. $75
Candy container, Independence Hall, bank, glass, dated. $150
Candy container, Independence Hall, dated 1776–1876. ....$395
Candy container, Liberty Bell, blue glass, early 20th century. $75
Candy container, Liberty Bell, clear glass, mid-20th century, original candy.
.... $35
Candy container, Liberty Bell, original tin closure, 3½ inches. $100
Candy container, papier-mâché, Independence Hall, early 20th century. ..$350
Candy container, Uncle Sam's hat, cardboard, 1930s, top lifts off from rim.
.... $45
Candy container, Uncle Sam, composition, removable base, 1930s. $175
Candy container, Uncle Sam, hat, milk glass, painted stars and stripes, tin
closure, early 20th century. $85
Candy container, Uncle Sam, papier-mâché, bottom opening, early 20th cen-
tury. $250
Candy container, Uncle Sam, papier-mâché, nodder, circa 1900. ....$275
Centerpiece, birthday cake, cardboard, firecrackers and flag around base, 12-
inch diameter, early 20th century. $50
Centerpiece, figure, Uncle Sam, carved wood with cloth costume, late 19th
century. $350
Centerpiece, figure, Uncle Sam, early 20th century, composition on wood base.
....$250
Centerpiece, top hat, striped cardboard with foil star banding, homemade, early
20th century. $25
Costume, Miss Liberty, red, white, and blue cotton stripes with banner and
stars and original crown, early 20th century. $75
Costume, Uncle Sam, striped trousers, cutaway jacket, top hat, beard, homemade, child size. $25

Decoration, candle-shaped cardboard, party favor, American flag paper fold-out, early 20th century. $15

Doorstop, Lady Liberty, liberty cap on pole, iron, black paint, early 20th century. $35

Flag, miniature, paper, party favors, package, early 20th century, Japanese. $10/pkg

Flask, Uncle Sam, figural, clear, early 20th century. $32

Game, Stars & Stripes, board, McLoughlin Bros., circa 1900. .... $990

Match holder, flag, shield shape, embossed "America," milk glass, early 20th century. $175

Mold, aluminum, Liberty Bell, mid-20th century. $10

Mold, chocolate, Liberty Bell, early 20th century, tin. $35

Mold, ice cream, flag, pewter hinged, 1930. .... $75

Needlework, motto, punched paper, "Long May It Wave," original frame. $250

Needlework, punched paper, 1776–1876, pictures of Lincoln and Washington, original frame. $350

Needlework, punched paper, rectangular shape, "Stars & Stripes," original grain painted frame, early 20th century. $275

Noisemaker, horn, lithographed tin, flags and bells, 1920. .... $10

Noisemaker, horn, red, white, and blue striped cardboard, wooden mouthpiece, 1930. .... $5

Noisemaker, rattle, lithographed tin, Uncle Sam's face, 1920. .... $10

Noisemaker, snapper, red, white, and blue crepe paper with gummed flag sticker. $5

Noisemaker, snapper, white crepe paper-covered cardboard, Liberty Bell in center, 1940, unused. $7

Noisemaker, whistle, cardboard and paper blow-out, red, white, and blue feather, 1930. .... $7

Nut cup, crepe paper with embossed cardboard shield and name tag. $5

Nut cup, double crepe paper frill, red, white, and blue, with attached name tag and gummed star, 1930. .... $5

Party favor, papier-mâché cigar with paper flag fold-out, early 20th century. $22

Plate, bicentennial, Jefferson, Declaration of Independence, 1973. .... $185

Plate, bicentennial, Wedgwood, American Independence, Victory, mid-20th century. $45

Plate, calendar, Liberty Bell, Philadelphia, transfer pottery, 1914. .... $35

Plate, eagle, fleur-de-lis, flag, early 20th century. $35

Platter, Liberty Bell, clear glass, early 20th century. $195

Postcard, Yankee Doodle, embossed cardboard, early 20th century. $10

Sheet music, "Stars & Stripes Forever." $10

Sheet music, "Yankee Doodle Dandy," James Cagney, 1931. .... $20

Spoon, Liberty Bell, sterling silver, early 20th century. $25

Streamers, crepe paper, red, white, and blue combination, cellophane package. $10/pkg

Tablecloth, Dennison, printed paper, red, white, and blue flags and Liberty Bells. $10

Table decoration, Liberty Bell, honeycomb tissue paper in red, white, and blue, cardboard base, 1930. .... $25

Halloween

Halloween, as we know it today, is the culmination of superstition and myth. The holiday, more than 1,300 years old, traces its origin to the Celtic or Druid peoples who celebrated the reaping of the harvest and thought this time of year marked the death of the old year and the beginning of the new one. The celebration included fire rites, where people and animals were burned to please the lord of the dead. Black cats were often sacrificed because they were thought to be able to be transformed into witches. With the decline of the pagan beliefs and the rise of religion as we know it, the people were told that the fire rites would protect them from the devil. Torches and bonfires were lit because it was thought that ghosts and witches feared the flames of the fire.

Some 800 years later, a festival known as All Saints Day was established on November 1 to coincide with the festival to remember the dead. The night before, October 31, was purported to be the time when the dead were to return and the believers were to welcome the ghosts. Also known as All Hallows Eve, the name was later changed to Halloween. This event, along with many of its attendant signs and symbols, was brought to this country by the Irish and Scottish immigrants.

The word "witch" derives from the Saxon word "wica," meaning wise one. Witches were originally revered for their magical prophecies. To assure more fertility for their animals, witches would masquerade as animals and gallop about straddling branches or broomsticks. This led, naturally, to tales of witches flying to their Sabbaths on broomsticks. Later, witches were thought to be messengers of the devil. In the eighteenth and nineteenth centuries, great witch hunts in Europe and America evolved from these myths which were thought to be true. The storybook witch, usually an old and ugly looking female, is a symbol of evil spirits.

Witches, believed to be able to change forms with a wave of a wand, were often aided by a cat, an owl or a bat. The cat was thought to help the witches with their magic powers and to be a form into which human beings were changed by evil spirits. In ancient Greece, the owl was believed to be a producer of evil. The weird whistle of the screech owl was thought by many to be the sound of the call of death. Bats, the only mammals to fly, are seldom seen at close range and only after dark. The frightening, strangely shaped hood which covers them in daylight resembles a witch's cape. Bats' abilities to fly around at darkest night portends some evil power. Their sharply pointed teeth are symbolic of the evil of witchery. Ghosts were believed to be the spirits or the disembodied souls of the dead that returned to their former homes looking for warmth and cheer. A fire was kept burning and the tables heaped with food. To displease the ghost was thought to be dangerous. Almost all religions and countries now have a day dedicated to the dead.

Skeletons and crossbones are the symbols of death. They also remind us that a holiday we now celebrate in fun was once a solemn day in remembrance of the dead.

The custom of using jack-o'-lanterns (pumpkins) as a means of light probably stems from the early lantern man who carried a lantern with its pale light into the countryside. Or perhaps it derived from the Irish legend of the poor soul named Jack who struck a very bad deal with the devil. He was doomed to carry a burning coal in a turnip for eternity. The practice of placing a candle in a turnip with carved faces and carrying the light around to frighten evil spirits was continued by the people of Ireland and Scotland. When the immigrants from these countries came to the United States, they found the pumpkin, with its bright orange color and its rounded shape, perfect for making jack-o'-lanterns.

Orange and black, the Halloween colors, also have their roots in the harvest festival and the festival of the dead. Orange is for strength and endurance, the color of the ripest grains and fruit. It is also the color of the flames that once rose from the fires on the dark hilltops to celebrate the fall harvest and frighten the evil spirits on All Hallows Eve. Black, the color of the night which turns familiar objects into frightening shapes, represents black magic and demonic influences. In its darkness lurks the threat of death from an evil spirit or a wild animal.

From the earliest times, people disguised themselves in the hopes that the demons who brought death and disaster would think them demons also and be frightened off. Pagans dressed in costume to represent the souls of the dead. Later, in the seventeenth and eighteenth centuries, church parishioners donned costumes for the same reasons.

By the latter part of the nineteenth century, All Hallows Eve was no longer considered a religious holiday in the United States. Parties were held at home. Pumpkins were carved, ghost stories were shared, and party goers bobbed and ducked for apples. Practical jokes were part of the fun for Halloween. Eggs were thrown. Cows were moved from field to field. Windows were soaped and children tried to say that ghosts were the responsible parties. From the latter part of the nineteenth until the early part of the twentieth century, and even today in this country, children roamed their neighborhoods dressed as ghosts and other mystical

Group of early 20th-century German Halloween dolls.
COURTESY OF
THERIAULT'S AUCTION.

forms to scare their neighbors. Today's costumed visitor with his trick-or-treat bag differs greatly from his earlier counterpart because today's visitor most often wears a store-bought costume and sometimes carries a box asking for funds for UNICEF.

Halloween is second only to Christmas as the most popular category of holiday collectible. While Christmas items were often saved as family heirlooms, Halloween decorations were not kept and were treated with far less respect. Children were allowed to play with Halloween decorations so fewer examples exist.

In 1887, Daniel Low in Salem, Massachusetts, the site of the original Salem witch trials, decided to issue sterling silver spoons depicting a witch on a broomstick. The pieces, made by the Durgin division of the Gorham Manufacturing Co., were so popular that they were followed by other versions of the spoon. The popularity of the Salem witch design inspired its use on scissors, hat pins, thimbles, bookmarks, brooches, stickpins, watch fobs, letter knives, tea strainers, and other flatware pieces. Unger Brothers, in business from 1872–1879 in Newark, New Jersey, manufactured a sterling silver bat pin that is coveted by both Halloween and Unger Bros. collectors.

Also at the end of the nineteenth century, ceramic souvenir plates and children's tea sets—transfer printed or decal decorated with flying witch designs—were made in England and Germany for the American market.

Most Halloween decorations are from the early part of the twentieth century (1900–1940) and, even though not technically antique items, are considered collectible. The primary production centers for the decorations were Germany, Japan, and the United States. In dating pieces, those marked ''Germany'' or ''Japan'' generally predate 1930. Pieces marked ''Made in Germany'' or ''Made in Japan'' were produced from

1930 until the beginning of World War II. Pieces marked "U.S. Zone Germany" date from 1945 to 1949.

There is an overwhelming abundance of Halloween memorabilia from the early part of the twentieth century. The following listings are merely an indication of the vastness of the market. They include papier-mâché and pressed cardboard candy containers, and glass, papier-mâché, and pressed cardboard lanterns, nodders, and mechanical toys. Noisemakers include cardboard and lithographed tin horns, tin and wooden whistles, and whistle blow-outs in cardboard and paper with colored feather detailing. Miniature accordions with symbolic representations on lithographed paper of Halloween motifs were another form of noisemaker believed to help scare evil spirits. Brightly lithographed cardboard and tin tambourines, cardboard and paper drums, printed tin clickers, and wooden and tin clackers and clappers in ratchet style with turned wooden handles produced a tremendously irritating noise. Another form of noise production was the lithographed tin noisemaker in double frying pan form with a wooden ball for maximum noise making. The lithographed noisemakers were almost always made by American companies. All of these pieces of memorabilia have decorations depicting the consistent themes of cats, witches, and/or ghosts reminiscent of the holiday.

Before World War II, Japan made bisque and celluloid figurines for decoration and use as candy containers in jack-o'-lantern and other Hal-

Group of early 20th-century Halloween collectibles. COURTESY OF SKINNER AUCTIONS.

loween forms to keep the spirit of the holiday. At your local five-and-dime store it was possible to buy clear glass full-figure pumpkin candy containers. Some were filled with sweets; others one could fill with homemade candies.

In the early 1900s, paper companies began manufacturing incredible quantities of printed paper decorations and party favors for an enthusiastic public. They issued a vast variety of color-coordinated design-matched paper goods for sale, all having the same motifs for a unified party look. When shopping at antiques shows, flea markets, auctions, tag sales, and antiques malls and centers, items to look for with all manner of Halloween leitmotif include: invitations, packaged gummed seals and stickers, place cards, printed paper plates, cups, napkins, nut cups, full-figure centerpieces in orange and black, trick-or-treat bags, lanterns, swags, festoons, and streamers. Nut cups, for example, can be found in full-figure cat or jack-o'-lantern shape made from papier-mâché with crepe paper accents, most with name cards attached.

From 1909 until 1934, one of the most prolific paper manufacturers and distributors, the Dennison Manufacturing Co. of Framingham, Massachusetts, a major supplier of party paper goods, produced a series of "Bogie" books. For 5 or 10 cents each, one would receive a party book full of suggestions for inviting guests, setting the table, decorating the room, and giving completely detailed directions on how to achieve a successful party. This series of special booklets indicated how your home should look for the party and which games to play and how to play them. Suggestions for types of parties included boy-and-girl costume parties, bridge parties, Halloween dances for schools, and even business-girl parties. "Bogie" books are eagerly sought by collectors because they give details about how to celebrate the holiday.

The 1931 Dennison Bogie book, *Hallowe'en Suggestions*, advises that when decorating for the holiday, use the mantelpiece, floor lamps, floor-model radios, and even the closets as backgrounds for skeletons and other apparitions. To achieve the desired effect, one must

clear the living room of much of the furniture; drape scraggly orange, gray, and black Crepe Paper Moss on chandeliers, pictures, and bric-a-brac; pin brightly colored designs of Decorated Crepe Paper over the window draperies as valances; add as many cardboard cats, witches, ghosts, and Jack-o'-Lanterns as you like and you will have created a real Hallowe'en spirit of weird gaiety for your party. Ghostly creatures should meet your guests at every turn. Make them over floor lamps or on dry mops and brooms. The attic may be called on to supply old coats, hats, and trousers to dress these weird creatures. Old sheets will, of course, be indispensable, while cut-outs of cats, witches, skulls, and Jack-o'-Lanterns will supply the heads. Natural branches stripped of their leaves are ideal for draping with Crepe Paper Moss. The more straggling and sparse it is, the more effective. These moss-covered branches are particularly attractive above windows or on an overhead light.

It was also suggested that chandeliers be decorated with orange and black crepe paper streamers tied in the center with a tassel suspended from the knot. Orange and black crepe paper festoons and streamers were criss-crossed throughout the house to add effect. Embossed black cat cardboard cut-outs could be used to decorate tops of windows or peer out the panes. A twig arched across the window could dangle cats or cut-out witches with cellophane fringe. In addition, Dennison manufactured paper printed with bats or jack-o'-lanterns and witches in cone-shaped hats, often with borders of large stars. Cardboard cut-outs depicting skeletons, witches, and black cats with accordion-style tissue paper bodies added to the ambiance of the evening's festivities. Pumpkin centerpieces were made by covering wires with orange crepe paper and then adding green crepe paper for the stem and leaves. Printed paper table covers were offered in dining and bridge table sizes, complete with matching napkins. Bridge tallies, and even coordinated invitations in matching sets, were common.

The company also made games for the at-home party. Exchanging ghost stories was always a highlight. Fortune telling was a constant theme for an evening's festivities. Ouija boards, crystal balls, mirror fortunes, and fortune hunts similar to scavenger hunts were the most popular. Halloween board games and puzzles, especially those intact and in their original box, command the highest prices.

During the first quarter of the twentieth century, there were 10,000 Dennison dealers in this country. Paper goods were mass produced to cover all party needs. In addition, at the Dennison stores dealers offered demonstrations on how to make the decorations and costumes. Many of us feel marketing concepts are new. Dennison and other companies, however, were actually ahead of their time by creating the goods and then creating a demand for these same goods they were producing.

Collectible costumes, homemade or store bought, from this time period include witches complete with their cone-shaped hats, skeletons, goblins, ghosts, devils, and black cats. Butterick, one of the many clothing pattern makers, offered a great selection of Halloween costumes. Dennison also made store-bought costumes, hats, and half- and full-face masks in addition to fake noses, teeth, beards, funny make-up, and wigs. Masks, also homemade and store bought, were in a variety of forms: rubber, embossed cardboard, papier-mâché or printed paper. Children borrowed mother's lipsticks, rouge, and food colorings. Burnt cork was used by many little boys to produce the beardlike effect of a hobo, one of the most popular costumes. Stuffed fabric toys from this same time period in familiar Halloween shapes are also collectible.

In Germany at the turn of the twentieth century, tin and pewter molds for ice cream or chocolate were often made with themes depicting pumpkins, witches on broomsticks or cats with arched backs. By the 1930s, the new aluminum molds were made in the same styles for Jell-O or aspic.

There are at least 5,000 different Halloween postcards in both cardboard and leather varieties from the early part of the twentieth century. Examples include those with squeakers, hold-to-light decoration, and even a Salem witch series. Cards depicted ghosts and witches, often as reflections of dead spirits. The black cat was also used, alone and as a companion to witches. Raphael Tuck, well known for his lithographed greeting cards, toys, and puzzles, produced a series of cards including witches, goblins, cats, and other symbols of the holiday. Many Halloween postcards portrayed small children chalking houses, ringing doorbells or stealing gates. They were also shown tapping on windows and ducking for apples.

Other collectible paper memorabilia for the Halloween enthusiast include comic books and *Saturday Evening Post* magazine covers from the early part of the twentieth century, both with Halloween themes; books about Halloween and witchcraft; and paper dolls in Halloween costumes. Also eagerly sought are embossed figural wall decorations such as skeletons, spiders, bats, and cats made by Dennison and other U.S. companies, as well as those made in Germany and Japan. Fans with tissue paper fold-outs depicting black cats, witches, bats, and folding garlands of orange and black tissue imported from Germany were popular.

Lantern lighting devices were commonly used by children in the early part of the twentieth century to light their way while trick-or-treating.

Left, *early 20th-century papier-mâché devil lantern;* right, *two early 20th-century cardboard lanterns.* COURTESY OF PAM AND CHRIS RUSSELL.

They were also used to decorate the windows and give a festive air to the house for the holiday. The lights, made in various materials including glass, pressed board, lithographed cardboard, and tin, depicted pumpkins, skulls, devils, owls, witches, and logs. Most of these are rare forms. At the turn of the twentieth century, pressed and hinged tin lanterns in the shape of a jack-o'-lantern and cut-out facial features and paint-decorated accents mounted on a wooden pole were used to light the way at costume parades. These are similar in function to parade lanterns used at political rallies. Neither lantern is commonly found today.

Molded wax candles appeared in the early part of the twentieth century to decorate the party table. They were made in a variety of forms including black cats, ghosts, and pumpkins. During the 1930s when figural Christmas lights became available, many were made depicting Halloween characters and symbols, especially by General Electric and other electric manufacturing companies. Most had silvered or painted decoration. Blown glass Christmas decorations depicting Halloween symbols were made in the latter part of the nineteenth and early part of the twentieth centuries, and they were most often used on the Christmas tree rather than at Halloween. (See discussion of Christmas ornaments for further information.) Since these decorations were fragile, few have survived.

Early twentieth-century cast iron objects having Halloween motifs include figural black cat bookends, iron candlesticks with applied cut-out sheet iron witches, and a painted figural doorstop depicting a young girl in a white ghost costume holding a pumpkin in front of her.

Advertising store displays from the early and middle parts of the twentieth centuries, especially those with known logos and familiar figures, are particularly rare and highly collectible. Few were produced; fewer were given out and then only to those merchants who had high sales

Early 20th-century weathervane depicting witch on broomstick.
PRIVATE COLLECTION.

volume. Popular examples to look for offer depictions of Dracula or The Munsters. Candy companies were especially well known for producing these store displays. If you can find and purchase examples produced for today's markets, they are bound to rise in value. Other popular collectibles from today's marketplace are the items produced by companies such as McDonald's, who recently offered a plastic full-figure lunch pail in the form of a pumpkin with black swing handle.

In the 1940s, molded plastic jewelry in the form of Halloween characters was sold in the dime store. Some pieces had movable parts, were worn to celebrate the holiday, and then were casually tossed to the back of a dresser drawer. Today these are the finds at a tag sale. Other good sources might be country hardware or general stores where, if you are lucky, you might find a pin or a group of pins on their original display card.

Specialized trick-or-treat bags for carrying one's loot or candy, most no more than 40 years old, have become popular collectibles. Since they were paper and thrown away after one use, few have survived and prices are expected to rise. Look for those with particular Halloween symbols, such as a little girl masquerading as a witch complete with cone-shaped hat, those with advertising logos and/or greetings for the season.

Medals and badges from specialized festivals and parades can be found at local tag sales and flea markets. Quite often they are mixed in with boxes of costume jewelry. Patinated metal or bronze badges in the form of pumpkin faces often bore the logo for the official badge of a particular town's celebration. Many of these celebrations are continued today, like the one in Anoka, Minnesota, the self-proclaimed Halloween capital of the world. Sponsored by the Chamber of Commerce, this festival is observed with a fitness run and walk, a bake-off, visits to a haunted house, costume contests, and other spirited events.

In today's throw-away society, although there is an incredible abundance of holiday decorations being produced to mirror the past, few will probably survive. In several years, many of these brightly colored holiday decorations might become the next newest collectible.

Halloween collectors might want to subscribe to the *Trick-or-Treat Trader*, a bimonthly newsletter for the enthusiast. Information can be obtained by writing C.J. Russell and The Halloween Queen, P.O. Box 499, Winchester, NH 03470.

Halloween Listings

Advertising, cardboard Heinz Haunted House, glows in dark. $6
Advertising, lunch pail, pumpkin form, plastic, McDonald's McGoblin. ... $15

Advertising, store display, cardboard, Happy Halloween from the Munsters, A & W Root Beer. $50
Advertising, store display, haunted house, cardboard, Hallmark, mid-20th century. .... .25
Apron, orange and black with ruffled edge, crepe paper, fair condition. ... $25
Badge, patinated metal, pumpkin head, 1902, Morristown, New Jersey, Halloween Festival. $20

Group of advertising posters. COURTESY OF PAM AND CHRIS RUSSELL.

Contemporary advertising display card and souvenir beer cans.
COURTESY OF PAM AND CHRIS RUSSELL.

Bag, trick-or-treat, molded plastic pumpkins, orange with black features, plastic handles, lot of five, mid-20th century. $25/5
Bag, trick-or-treat, paper, lithographed, pumpkin head and Happy Halloween, 1940. .... $18
Bag, trick-or-treat, paper, printed with young girl dressed as witch, early 20th century. $25
Bank, skeleton, in coffin, tin, Japan, mid-20th century. $45
Bell, cat and witch figures, tin, painted, early 20th century. $30
Book, Bogie, Dennison, 1923. .... $25
Book, Bogie, Dennison, 1931. .... $25
Book, Bogie, Dennison, 1933, party ideas, fair condition. $18
Book, Charlie Brown's Pumpkin Carols, mid-20th century. $10

Early 20th-century Halloween party books. COURTESY OF PAM AND CHRIS RUSSELL.

*Pair of early 20th-century iron
witch candlesticks, $250/pr.*

Book, Fortune Telling, early 20th century, hard-bound, fair condition. $18
Bookend, witch on broom, cast iron, early 20th century. $50
Booklet, Pranks & Parties, paper, 1927. .... $18
Bridge tallies, witch with cauldron, paper, 1930, package. $5
Broom, witch, paper and wood, fair condition, repaired, 6¼ inches tall. .. $25
Can, beer, Halloween symbols made for Festival in Anoka, Minnesota, 1979.
.... $10
Candle, black cat and crescent moon, 1940. .... $15
Candle, black cat, arched back, 1930s. $10
Candle, cat, small size. $5
Candle, ghost, holding pumpkin, 1940. ....$7
Candle, pumpkin face, painted features, 1940. ....$5
Candle, witch with broom, 1930. .... $10
Candle holder, pumpkin, cardboard, tissue face, early 20th century. $75
Candle holder, pumpkin, papier-mâché, 1920s. $28
Candle holder, skull, cardboard, tissue face, early 20th century. $75
Candles, pumpkins, orange, set of four in original box. $10/set
Candlesticks, witch, pair, riding on broomsticks, cast and sheet iron, circa 1940.
.... $250/pr
Candy box, pumpkin with corn ears, mid-20th century, 10½ inches. $25
Candy box, pumpkin, stuffed crepe paper, 3 inches high. $25
Candy box, witch eating black cat, German, papier-mâché, long drawer in box,
crank handle and watch witch eat cat, good condition, 5½ inches × 5 inches.
.... $375
Candy box, witch head, papier-mâché, early 20th century. $450
Candy box, witch stirring cauldron on top, cardboard, 1930. .... $75
Candy box, witch with black cat, German, papier-mâché, good condition, 4
inches high. $50
Candy box, witch with black cat, papier-mâché, hat crazed condition, early 20th
century, 4 inches high. $50
Candy box, cardboard, lithographed Halloween decorations, 1930s. $45
Candy box, devil, German, cloth dressed, papier-mâché, good condition, 6
inches. $75
Candy box, ghost, cloth dressed, papier-mâché, missing base, good condition,
6¼ inches. $60
Candy box, goblin, stuffed crepe paper figure, good condition, 4¾ inches.
.... $35
Candy box, Halloween decorated, cardboard, 1930s. $15

Candy box, hat box, lithographed paper, composition pumpkin head, stick pin inside, Germany, 1930. .... $95

Candy box, pumpkin head goblin, German, cloth dressed, papier-mâché, good condition, 5¾ inches. $65

Candy box, pumpkin head, Japan, crepe paper, 1940. .... $25

Candy boxes, pumpkin head in suitcase form, lithographed cardboard, group of four. $125/4

Candy container, black cat, painted, composition, blown glass eyes, closed mouth, 3 inches high. $75

Candy container, candle in holder, lithographed paper on cardboard, early 20th century, 5½ inches high. $250

Candy container, black cat, full-figure papier-mâché. $70

Candy container, black cat, glass eyes. $85

Candy container, black cat, good luck, early 20th century, 4 inches high. $75

Candy container, black cat, hard plastic, orange decoration. $5

Candy container, black cat, with creature on arched back, 4 inches high. $195

Candy container, cat, cardboard, early 1900s. $35

Candy container, cat, cloth-covered cardboard, 1920s. $65

Candy container, cat, cloth-covered cardboard, with blown glass eyes, early 20th century. $150

Candy container, cat, papier-mâché, bottom opens, early 20th century. ...$150

Candy container, cat, standing, blown glass eyes, papier-mâché, German, early 20th century. $195

Candy container, devil's head, papier-mâché, 1930s. $225

Candy container, devil's head, papier-mâché, bottom opens, 1920s. $450

Candy container, ghost, papier-mâché, early 20th century. $150

Candy container, jack-o'-lantern, composition, early 20th century. $75

Candy container, lot of three black cats, painted composition glass eyes, circa 1930, 3 inches. $180/3

Candy container, mushroom, painted face, papier-mâché, early 20th century, 4 inches. $165

Candy container, owl, papier-mâché, blown glass eyes, painted feathers, 1920. .... $200

Candy container, pumpkin head bell, painted glass, tin closure, good condition, 3¾ inches high. $360

Candy container, pumpkin head witch, painted glass, tin closure, very fine, 4¾ inches high. $320

Candy container, pumpkin man, painted plaster, 2½ inches high. $120

Candy container, pumpkin on black cat, hard plastic, 1950, United States. $10

Candy container, pumpkin, boy, painted plaster, missing cardboard base, 3½ inches high. $130

Candy container, pumpkin, molded cardboard, 1940. .... $65

Candy container, pumpkin, plastic, mid-20th century. $5

Candy container, vegetable head, 1930. .... $125

Candy container, vegetable head, papier-mâché, 1930s, German. $200

Candy container, witch face in tree trunk, early 20th century. $2,000

Candy container, witch head with hat, papier-mâché, early 20th century. $175

Candy container, witch head, papier-mâché, 1920. .... $150

Group of early 20th-century candy containers. COURTESY OF PAM AND CHRIS RUSSELL AND SKINNER AUCTIONS.

Group of early and mid-20th-century candy containers and baskets. PRIVATE COLLECTION.

Early 20th-century candy container and papier-mâché and glass lanterns. COURTESY OF PAM AND CHRIS RUSSELL.

Left, *early 20th-century papier-mâché candy container depicting witch on jack-o'-lantern;* right, *early 20th-century witch candy container.*

COURTESY OF JOAN AND ALLAN LEHNER.

Candy container, witch roly-poly, 1920. ....$150

Candy container, witch with pumpkin head, red dress, white apron, missing broom, fair condition, 6 inches. $150

Candy container, witch, cauldron and broom, full figure on cardboard base with crepe paper. $95

Candy container, witch, glass. $450

Candy container, witch, papier-mâché, 1930. ....$125

Candy container, witch, papier-mâché, early 20th century, opens on base. $125

Candy container, witch, papier-mâché, with hat and broom, head lifts off, 1930s, Germany, height 6 inches. $275

Candy container, witch/vegetable person, papier-mâché, hat, marked "Germany." $150

Candy containers, ghost, witch and pumpkin, lithographed cardboard, poor condition. $75

Card, tally, black cat scene. $3

Card, tally, two pumpkins. $3

Card, tally, witch on broom. $3

Centerpiece, ghost, cardboard with honeycomb tissue base, 1930. .... $25

Centerpiece, pumpkin, honeycomb tissue paper fold-out. $15

Centerpiece, skeleton, coated cardboard, seated on tissue fold-out base, 9 inches high, 1920. ....$35

Centerpiece, witch, cardboard and tissue paper inserts, circa 1940. .... $20

Clacker, cat, arched back, pan shape, wood, early 20th century. $15

Clacker, black cat, head, crepe paper trim, wood, German, early 20th century. $75

Clapper, witch on broom, painted wood, 8 inches. $45

Clicker, Mickey Mouse, lithographed tin, 1930. ....$65

Cookie cutter, ghost, tin, early 20th century. $5

Cookie cutter, pumpkin, early 20th century. $3

Cookie cutter, witches and cats, set, mid-20th century. $10

Costume, Bewitched, original package, 1950. ....$20

Costume, bow tie, witch decoration, circa 1940. ....$10

Costume, Casper the Ghost, original box, 1950. ....$15

Costume, devil, crepe paper and cloth, rubber mask, 1940. ....$25

Costume, fortune teller, homemade, 1940. ....$30

Costume, ghost, homemade, sheet, with cut-outs. $5

Costume, lily, crepe paper, Dennison, 1930s. $20

Costume, maid, apron and cap, crepe paper and fabric, homemade. $15

Costume, martian, with papier-mâché head, homemade, 1970. .... $15

Costume, circus clown, mask, homemade, child's, 1930. ....$35

Costume, Peter Rabbit, original box, mid-20th century. $15

Costume, Snoopy, original box, mid-20th century. $15

Costume, Statue of Liberty, crepe paper, cardboard crown, Dennison, homemade, circa 1950. ....$25

Costume, television set, homemade, cardboard with antenna, 1970s. $35

Costume, Wicked Witch, from the *Wizard of Oz*, original box. $50

Costume, witch, with broom and mask, original box, 1920. ....$20

Costume, witch, crepe paper, Dennison, early 20th century. $25

Costume, Zorro, original box, mid-20th century. $25

Doll, cat, bisque socket head, side-glancing green googly eyes, five-piece gray papier-mâché body, marked "Heubach Germany." $1,200

Doll, Dracula, dressed in tails, vinyl, 12½ inches high. $75

Doll, witch, German, bisque, socket head, depicting scowling older woman, inset eyes, marked "Hexe 15/0, Cuno & Otto Dessel," wearing maroon skirt, black blouse, apron, orange felt cape and cap. $750

Doorstop, cat, full figure, cast iron, black, painted features, 10 inches high. $95

Doorstop, Halloween girl, cast iron, painted, early 20th century. $2,800

Fan, orange tissue fold-out, black cat design, Germany, 1920. .... $20

Fan, orange tissue fold-out, black witch with cat and bats, wooden handle, Germany, 1920. .... $20

Fan, orange, black, paper lithographed, German, early 20th century. $22

Favor, cat, cardboard with crepe paper, full figure. $10

Favor, confetti pouch, handpainted cat's head, double crepe paper frill. $35

Favor, crackers (snappers), crepe paper with owl decoration, 1940. ....$5

Favor, crackers (snappers), crepe paper, black cat and witch decals, box of 12. .... $75/12

Favor, hat, orange cardboard, printed black Halloween scene, Germany, 4 inches high. $10

Favor, noisemaker rattle, full-figure ghost, paper, stick, and cardboard construction, handpainted face, marked "Pi Beta Phi–Delta Tau Delta," 1917, 10 inches high. $125

Favor, skull, papier-mâché, early 20th century. $22

Favor, snapper with ghost head and pumpkin ends containing crepe paper hat, snapper, and verse. $35

Figure, jack-o'-lantern, head—painted pressed board, tissue, some burn damage; body—painted papier-mâché, gessoed, 6 inches high. $425

Figure, pumpkin girl, painted plaster, 4¾ inches high. $160

Figure, witch, pumpkin head, holding broom, papier-mâché, paper hat, straw broom and hair, 7 inches high. $100

Game, Fortune Telling, lithographed paper, orange and black. $15

Game, Ouija Board, lithographed cardboard, original box, 1930. .... $45

Game, ring toss, lithographed paper, Halloween symbols, original box. ..$425

Garland, folding, orange and black tissue with cardboard pumpkin heads and witch cut-outs, German, 8-inch length. $15

Garland, folding, plain orange and black tissue. $5

Goblin, nodder, boy, dressed, painted papier-mâché, wood base, 6¼ inches high. $150

Goblin, nodder, Oriental face, painted papier-mâché with cloth leaves, vegetable body, painted plaster-cracked head, 8 inches tall. $250

Hat, clown, cloth, good condition, 13 inches high. $10

Hat, party, lithographed paper, black cat and crescent moon, 12 inches high. $25

Hat, witch, cardboard, 1930. .... $10

Hat, witch, tin whimsey, crimp decorated with bow and plume, together with sword, circa 1850. ....$1,900

Horn, blow-out, cardboard, lithographed cat, Dennison, 1940s. $25

Invitation, owl, full figure. $2

Invitation, pumpkin and witches on broom. $3

Invitations, witch and black cat, 1940, package. $5

Jack-o'-lantern, painted glass, tin closure, 3¾ inches high. $70

Jack-o'-lantern, baby head on vegetable body, painted papier-mâché, gessoed, head damage, 5¾ inches high. $140

Lithographed paper party invitations and postcards, early 20th century.
COURTESY OF PAM AND CHRIS RUSSELL.

Jack-o'-lantern, black cat, painted and flocked papier-mâché, gessoed, paper face and ribbon, wire bale, 4 inches tall. $275

Jack-o'-lantern, black cat, painted pressed board, tissue, wire bale, crepe paper bow tie, 4½ inches tall. $110

Jack-o'-lantern, black pumpkin with ears, painted pressed board, tissue, wire bale, 3½ inches tall. $90

Jack-o'-lantern, black pumpkin, painted pressed board, tissue, no bale, some top edges burned, 2½ inches tall. $80

Jack-o'-lantern, cat, coleslaw body, cloth ears, tissue, wire bale, head has melted entire back and some of front, 4½ inches high. $150

Jack-o'-lantern, cat, painted pressed board, tissue, wire bale, 5 inches high. $210

Jack-o'-lantern, cat, papier-mâché, 1940. ....$10

Jack-o'-lantern, devil, painted papier-mâché and tissue, wire bale, 2¾ inches tall. $180

Jack-o'-lantern, devil, painted pressed board, tissue, wire bale, large burn damage section in back, 4½ inches high. $150

Jack-o'-lantern, devil, painted pressed board, tissue, wire bale, one ear tip ripped but there, 3½ inches high. $200

Jack-o'-lantern, laughing, molded cardboard, orange, 5-inch diameter. ... $52

Jack-o'-lantern, lot of two, papier-mâché, paper faces, 2¾ inches high and 5½ inches high. $27/2

Jack-o'-lantern, lot of two, papier-mâché, paper faces, 5 inches high and 3¾ inches high. $20/2

Jack-o'-lantern, on top of accordion, orange papier-mâché, Germany. ... $200

Jack-o'-lantern, painted glass, some flaking to paint, 3 inches high. $50

Jack-o'-lantern, painted tin, three dimensional, candle holder inside, stick, 9-inch head is collapsible, very good. $230

Jack-o'-lantern, papier-mâché, good condition, 1940, 7 inches high. $20

Jack-o'-lantern, papier-mâché, original paper eyes, 4 inches high. $45

Jack-o'-lantern, papier-mâché, paper face and base, excellent, 5½ inches high. $75

Jack-o'-lantern, papier-mâché, paper face, base missing, excellent, 3¾ inches high. $60

Jack-o'-lantern, pressed paper, Germany, 1940. .... $25

Jack-o'-lantern, pumpkin with ears, painted pressed board, replaced tissue, 6 inches high. $140

Jack-o'-lantern, pumpkin, painted board, tissue, wire bale, 3½ inches high. $70

Jack-o'-lantern, pumpkin, painted egg carton-type papier-mâché, tissue, wire bale, 5 inches high. $210

Jack-o'-lantern, pumpkin, painted papier-mâché, gessoed, tissue, small face repair, 2¼ inches high. $55

Jack-o'-lantern, pumpkin, painted papier-mâché, tissue, wire bale, 3 inches high. $70

Jack-o'-lantern, pumpkin, painted pressed board, tissue, wire bale, 4¼ inches high. $45

Jack-o'-lantern, pumpkin, painted pressed board, tissue, wire bale, 4¾ inches high. $65

Jack-o'-lantern, pumpkin, painted pressed board, tissue, wire bale, 6 inches high. $120

Jack-o'-lantern, pumpkin, painted pressed board, tissue, wire bale, 7½ inches high. $200

Jack-o'-lantern, pumpkin, painted pressed steel, wire handle, tissue, pumpkin 5¾ inches high. $190

Jack-o'-lantern, pumpkin, painted pressed steel, wire handle, stamped "Patented May 13, 1902, Toledo Metal Sign Co.," 7 inches high, tissue missing. $650

Jack-o'-lantern, pumpkin, very thin paper on stained tin frame, fragile and some rips, 4 inches high. $95

Jack-o'-lantern, red devil with horns, painted pressed board, tissue, wire bale, horns off but there, 3½ inches high. $80

Jack-o'-lantern, skull, painted plaster, tissue, 3 inches high. $300

Jack-o'-lantern, tissue paper face, papier-mâché, 7½ inches high. $35

Jack-o'-lantern, tree stump, pressed board with rough flocking, tissue, wire bale, 6 inches high. $160

Jack-o'-lantern, two-face, papier-mâché, early 20th century. $175

Jack-o'-lantern, two, papier-mâché, worn orange paint, 4½ inches and 5½ inches high. $75/2

Jack-o'-lantern, two, papier-mâché, worn orange paint, 4½ and 5½ inches high, mid-20th century. $75/2

Jack-o'-lantern, watermelon, painted papier-mâché, gesso, tissue, wire bale, 4¼ inches wide. $375

Jack-o'-lantern, wire handle, papier-mâché, Germany, 5½ inches × 4 inches. $45

Jack-o'-lantern, with scowl, painted papier-mâché, gessoed, tissue, 2¾ inches high. $250

Jack-o'-lantern, with vegetable body and nodding head, composition, Germany, 1920, 3 inches high. $175

Jack-o'-lanterns, eight, papier-mâché, some damage. $150/8

Jewelry, pin, black cat, hard plastic. $15

Jewelry, pin, devil's head, hard plastic. $15

Late 19th-century Unger Bros.
bat and moon pin, $900.

Mid-20th-century stickpins
and bow ties. COURTESY OF
PAM AND CHRIS RUSSELL.

Jewelry, pin, owl, hard plastic. $15
Jewelry, pin, owl, witch, pumpkin, composition. $10/each
Jewelry, pin, pumpkin face, composition, German, 3 inches high. $12
Jewelry, pin, sterling silver, bat and moon, Unger Bros. $900
Jewelry, pin, witch, hard plastic. $15
Jewelry, stick pin, cotton pumpkin with hat, 3 inches high. $8
Lamp, pumpkin on black cat on molded base with skeletons, orange plastic, opening for light bulb, 1950. .... $15
Lantern, bats over moon, pressed paper, Germany, 1930s. $85
Lantern, black cat on top, composition, early 20th century. $65
Lantern, black cat, with arched back, pressed cardboard, 1920. .... $35
Lantern, box-shaped cardboard with skulls on sides, wire handle, mid-20th century. $75
Lantern, cat face, papier-mâché, early 20th century. $25

Group of early 20th-century lanterns. COURTESY OF DON MEHRER.

Left, *early 20th-century cardboard and glass lanterns;* right, *group of Halloween lanterns.* COURTESY OF PAM AND CHRIS RUSSELL.

Lantern, cat face, pressed cardboard, black, with wire handle, Germany, 1930. .... $75

Lantern, cat, full figure, papier-mâché with tissue paper, Germany, 1920. .... $200

Lantern, cat's head, black, molded cardboard, tissue paper-painted eyes, wire bale handle, 1930s. $225

Lantern, cat's head, uncolored molded cardboard, painted features, bale handle. $100

Lantern, cat, black cardboard with tissue face. $35

Lantern, child's, pumpkin head, glass, battery operated, 1940. .... $65

Lantern, child's, skull head, molded glass, battery operated, 1940. .... $45

Lantern, devil jack-o'-lantern, full figure, red papier-mâché, early 20th century, Germany. $650

Lantern, devil's head, pressed cardboard, early 20th century. $85

Lantern, jack-o'-lantern, double faced, papier-mâché, glass eyes, early 20th century. $500

Lantern, jack-o'-lantern, tin, no stick, paint touched up, 1900–1908. .... $400

Lantern, jack-o'-lantern, watermelon shape, circa 1920, German, 3 inches high. $400

Lantern, owl, frosted glass, battery operated, 1940. .... $35

Lantern, owl, molded colored paper, tissue eyes and mouth, wire handle, missing nose. $95

Lantern, pumpkin-head goblin, papier-mâché, cloth decorations, fine, 5¼ inches high. $220

Left, *tin parade lantern;* right, *group of glass lanterns, early 20th century.* COURTESY OF PAM AND CHRIS RUSSELL.

Group of mid-20th-century plastic Halloween collectibles. COURTESY OF PAM AND CHRIS RUSSELL.

Lantern, pumpkin shape, papier-mâché, 1920s. $150
Lantern, pumpkin, devil jack-o'-lantern, papier-mâché, 1910. ....$145
Lantern, pumpkin, glass, mid-20th century, fine condition. $35
Lantern, pumpkin, glass, mid-20th century. $50
Lantern, pumpkin, molded glass, 1940. ....$45
Lantern, skull, milk glass head, battery operated, 1940, 4½ inches high. . $45
Lantern, skull, pressed board with tissue paper face, wire handle, early 20th century. $75
Lantern, witch head, painted papier-mâché, gessoed, tissue, wire bale handle, John Wanamaker label, 3¼ inches high. $425
Letter knife, Salem witch, sterling silver. $125
Light bulb, jack-o'-lantern with painted decoration. $25
Lot, including mask, black face and black head, gauze; red wig, green mask; black boa; party hat; Palmer Cox Brownie mask. $15/all
Lot of items, 20th century, including costumes, hats, masks, papier-mâché black cat lantern, jack-o'-lanterns, tin candy mold, noisemakers, decoration, paper goods, some lot damage. $200/all
Lot of items, 20th century, including costumes, masks, hats, Witches Game, papier-mâché pumpkins, cats, noisemakers, paper decorations, some lot damage. $200/all
Lot of items, 20th century, including lithographed tin jack-o'-lantern, honeycomb crepe paper pumpkin, costumes, masks, hats, tambourine and other noisemakers, paper goods and decorations, some lot damage. $200/all
Lot of items, 20th century, including papier-mâché cat lantern and ten jack-o'-lanterns in assorted sizes, masks, noisemakers, place cards, folding paper lanterns, some lot wear. $275/all
Marionette, witch, 1930. ....$35

Mask, clown face, papier-mâché, painted features, early 20th century. $35
Mask, Harlequin, half-mask, satin. $5
Mask, Pinocchio, sized netting, early 20th century. $15
Mask, robot, silver paper, mid-20th century. $15
Mask, skeleton, painted cloth, early 20th century. $25
Mask, skull head, German, papier-mâché, very fine, 10 inches high. $70
Mask, witch, printed paper, mid-20th century. $20
Masks, lot of seven, including Snow White, two witches, two Docs, Grumpy, Dopey, lithographed paper. $45/all
Masks, lot of three, including Daisy Mae, Topstone rubber; witch, German, painted papier-mâché; black face with bow tie, rubber. $25/3
Masks, lot of, including bald head with hair fringe, man with moustache and goatee, Oriental with black straw hat, bum with cigar, rubber, papier-mâché, cloth. $5/all
Mold, cake, aluminum, witch, full figure, mid-20th century. $10
Mold, chocolate, four witches, early 20th century, German. $150
Mold, ice cream, pumpkin, early 20th century, iron. $50
Mold, witch on broom, tin, late 19th century, German. $125
Nodder, devil, papier-mâché, very good, 6¾ inches high. $70
Nodder, pumpkin figure, German label, painted papier-mâché, gessoed head, solid painted plaster body on wood base, head cracked in back, 4½ inches high. $140
Nodder, skull head goblin, German, papier-mâché, very fine, 8¾ inches high. $100
Noisemaker, accordion, cardboard with lithographed paper witch motif. .. $28
Noisemaker, black cat on tin pan, wooden handle, 3 inches. $15
Noisemaker, black cat with movable legs, papier-mâché and wood, 8 inches high. $70
Noisemaker, cats, witches, ghosts, lithographed tin pan, wooden handle. . $10
Noisemaker, cigarette whistle, two-tone orange and black, shredded paper end. $15
Noisemaker, clappers, wood and metal, square shape. $15
Noisemaker, clicker, lithographed tin, Halloween symbols. $10
Noisemaker, clicker, lithographed tin, rectangular shape. $10
Noisemaker, horn with cat head cut-out, blow-out. $25
Noisemaker, horn, lithographed cardboard and papier-mâché, 1930. .... $10
Noisemaker, horn, lithographed paper and wood, Halloween symbols, 1920. ....$18

Early 20th-century witch molds.

Early 20th-century tin clickers and frying pan clappers. COURTESY OF PAM
AND CHRIS RUSSELL.

Noisemaker, horns, Halloween symbols, lithographed, tin, dozen, original box,
1930s. $50/set
Noisemaker, orange, black, and white, yellow clapper, paper over tin. $10
Noisemaker, pumpkin head and goblin, composition on lithographed paper ac-
cordion, 6 inches high. $50
Noisemaker, pumpkin head, molded cardboard with paper blow-out. $45
Noisemaker, pumpkin, papier-mâché and wood, 9 inches high. $27
Noisemaker, ratchet-style wooden with molded composition cat at top, 1940s.
....$150
Noisemaker, ratchet, composition cat's head. $85
Noisemaker, ratchet, lithographed paper with witch and cat, wooden handle,
1920. ....$25
Noisemaker, ratchet, lithographed tin, Halloween symbols. $15
Noisemaker, ratchet, wood with composition pumpkin head, Germany, 1930.
....$85
Noisemaker, ratchet, wooden base, full-figure witch, red and white paper clothes,
marked "Germany." $1,200
Noisemaker, ratchet, wooden, with molded composition witch at top, 1940s.
....$150
Noisemaker, rattle, pumpkin, cardboard, 1920. ....$75
Noisemaker, rotating, printed tin head of witch. $20
Noisemaker, rotating, printed tin, "Happy Halloween." $15
Noisemaker, shaker, cylindrical lithographed tin, black cat, wooden handle.
....$15
Noisemaker, tambourine, cardboard, printed decoration. $12
Noisemaker, tambourine, children dancing around pumpkin, lithographed tin,
orange and black, early 20th century. $45
Noisemaker, tambourine, lithographed cardboard with tin inserts, print of
pumpkin. $20
Noisemaker, tambourine, lithographed tin, orange and black cat motif, 1930s.
....$30
Noisemaker, whistle, cardboard with papier-mâché, printed paper, 1920. . $15
Noisemaker, whistle, cat, lithographed paper with blow-out. $15
Noisemaker, witch with cauldron, lithographed tin, frying pan shape. $10

Noisemaker, witch's face, orange and black, lithographed tin frying pan shape. $10
Noisemaker, witch, papier-mâché, wooden, clacker. $45
Noisemaker, witch, pumpkin face, lithographed tin, early 20th century. ... $35
Noisemaker, tambourine, witch design, lithographed tin, 1930. .... $28
Novelties, group, German including caricature expressions, modeled children's clothes, girl holding black cat, marked "Germany," bisque figure of googly eyed boy standing next to Halloween jack-o'-lantern marked "Ges Gesch Germany 8045," generally excellent condition, circa 1920, unusual, imaginative. $400/lot
Novelties, pair, German, each is one-piece papier-mâché head and torso, suggestive of jack-o'-lantern, generally excellent condition, original hanging loops suggest original use as Halloween ornaments, figures are imaginative and well preserved. $300/pr
Novelty, cake decorations, pumpkins, devils, skulls, paper, mid-20th century. $10/lot
Nut basket, twisted crepe paper, two-tone handle, orange and black ribbon. $5
Nut cup, crepe paper, large devil's head cut-out. $10
Nut cup, jack-o'-lantern, crepe paper and cardboard, 1940. .... $35
Nut cup, pumpkin, with skeleton decoration, Dennison, 3 inches high. $10
Nut cup, ruffled crepe paper, Halloween cat cut-out on back. $10
Nut cup, two-tone ruffled crepe paper, handpainted doll Halloween costume. $25
Nut cup, witch's kettle, pressed cardboard, 1940. ....$5
Nut tray, double-pointed paper on 5-inch diameter plate with doily. $20
Nut tray, printed paper, Halloween symbols, 3½-inch diameter, 1920s. ... $15
Pencil, handpainted witch's head, pointed hat and broom. $25
Photograph, children's costume party, 1940s. $30
Photograph, Halloween parade at school, 1940s. $35
Place card, pipe cleaners, handpainted head and place card. $5
Place card, witch and bats. $2
Postcard, girl with pumpkin, embossed and lithographed, 1930. .....;.......$7
Postcard, "Happy Halloween," witch on broom, early 20th century. $10
Postcard, jack-o'-lantern, embossed cardboard, early 20th century. $5
Postcard, jack-o'-lantern, hold-to-light. $25
Postcard, skeleton at door, children in background. $10
Postcard, "The Fortune Teller." $5
Pumpkin head, roly-poly, painted papier-mâché, cloth-covered body, end of one hand missing, 2 inches high. $85

Salem witch ceramic plate; partial pottery tea set. COURTESY OF PAM AND CHRIS RUSSELL.

Puppet, witch hand, cloth and composition, mid-20th century. $15

Puppet, witch, late 19th century. $275

Puppets, hand, witch, pumpkin and ghost, homemade, cloth and wood, mid-20th century. $50/all

Rattle, pumpkin, papier-mâché, circa 1920. .... $125

Skeleton, cardboard with honeycomb tissue connectors, 1950s. $10

Skeleton, cardboard, 23 inches × 23 inches. $12

Skeleton, on base, painted papier-mâché, gessoed head, solid painted plaster body, spring neck and arms, cardboard base, spring mechanical flapping jaw with paper watermelon plunger, 4¼ inches high. $220

Snow dome, haunted house. $22

Sparkler, lithograph tin, witch and cat motif, 1930s. $75

Spiders, lot of four, composition, gessoed, glass eyes, spring legs. $20/4

Spoon, Salem witch, sterling silver. $35

Squeaker, black cat, painted papier-mâché, tail missing, squeaker not working, 3½ inches wide. $95

Stickers, labels, lot of assorted Dennison depicting pumpkins, owls, bats. $75/all

Streamers, crepe paper, orange and black stripes, cellophane package. $10

Tablecloth, printed paper, orange with black witches and cats. $10

Table decoration, basket with pumpkin facial features, coated orange paper, handle forms head. $75

Table decoration, cat, arched back, full-figure composition, 1940s. $75

Table decoration, black cat, arched back, papier-mâché, early 20th century. $55

Table decoration, black cat, full-figure cardboard with tissue fold-out, 1940. .... $15

Table decoration, black cat, grinning, pumpkin on back, 4 inches. $125

Table decoration, black cat, sitting, German, painted composition, blown glass eyes, wire spring neck, 3 inches high. $55

Table decoration, jack-o'-lantern, watermelon, papier-mâché, 1920. .... $65

Table decoration, owl, brown cardboard, 3 inches. $15

Table decoration, full-figure pumpkin, chenille, 1930s. $1,250

Table decoration, pumpkin, crepe paper on cardboard base, Dennison. ... $35

Table decoration, pumpkin, fold-out honeycomb tissue paper, mid-20th century. $10

Table decoration, pumpkin, hard plastic, 1970s. $10

Table decoration, pumpkin, papier-mâché, 1920. .... $35

Table decoration, skeleton, wearing top hat, composition, marked "Germany." $45

Table decoration, witch with broom, composition, 1920. .... $50

Thimble, Salem witch, sterling silver. $450

Torch, parade, pumpkin shape, tin, with cut-out face, 1920s. $275

Torch, pumpkin face, molded and cut tin, orange with black outlining, wooden handle, early 20th century. $475

Torch, pumpkin tin, missing stick, worn paint, 1920. .... $250

Toy, jumping jack, pumpkin shaped, wooden, 1920s. $35

Toy, jumping jack, witch with black cat, wooden, 1920. .... $40

Toy, jumping jack, witch, 1920. .... $25

Toy, jumping jack, witch, wooden, 1920. .... $35

Toy, top, lithographed tin, witches and cats, orange and black wooden handle, mid-20th century. $25

Above, *early 20th-century molded cardboard rattle;* right, *early 20th-century sheet music.* COURTESY OF PAM AND CHRIS RUSSELL.

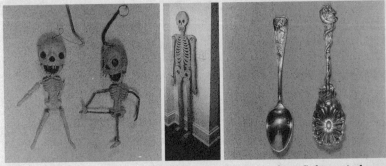

Left, *early 20th-century skeletons;* right, *sterling silver Salem witch spoons.* COURTESY OF PAM AND CHRIS RUSSELL.

Tambourines; lithographed tin noisemakers. COURTESY OF PAM AND CHRIS RUSSELL.

Left, *early 20th-century embossed cardboard wall decoration.* COURTESY OF JOAN AND ALLAN LEHNER. **Right,** *group of early and mid-20th-century embossed cardboard wall decorations.* COURTESY OF PAM AND CHRIS RUSSELL.

Toy, witch jack-in-the-box, lithographed paper over cardboard, 1920. .....$225
Toy, witch jumping jack, wooden, painted orange, black. $35
Wall decoration, black cat, embossed cardboard, circa 1940. ....$10
Wall decoration, black cat, green eyes, 12 inches high. $10
Wall decoration, devil, full figure, embossed paper, German. $18
Wall decoration, devil, pressed cardboard, heavily embossed, 15½ inches high. $18
Wall decoration, jack-o'-lantern, cardboard cut-out, black, orange tissue, two-sided, 2 inches × 6 inches. $54
Wall decoration, man with pumpkin head and smiling face, embossed paper. $15
Wall decoration, musician, full figure with pumpkin head, embossed cardboard. $22
Wall decoration, pressed cardboard cat in lady's clothing, marked "Germany," 20 inches. $35
Wall decoration, pumpkin, embossed lithographed cardboard, happy face, mid-20th century. $5
Wall decoration, skeleton, cardboard with tissue inserts. $15
Wall decoration, witch stirring cauldron, black cats, circa 1940. ....$20
Wall decoration, witch with broom, cut-out full-figure embossed cardboard, orange and black. $15
Wall decoration, witch, pressed paper, Germany. $35
Weathervane, witch and black cat, flat copper cut-out, 1930s, homemade. $950
Weathervane, witch on broom, sheet iron, late 19th century, American, with original paint. $2,500
Witch, flying with broom, pressed paper, 1940. ....$25

Thanksgiving

Thanksgiving, a uniquely American holiday, was created in 1621 by the Pilgrims, who rested from their chores to celebrate a three-day harvest festival in Plymouth, Massachusetts. Even though the holiday continues as one of thankfulness today, it was not until 1863 that President Abraham Lincoln declared Thanksgiving a national holiday, probably in an effort to unite the disparate states.

Decorations from the earliest celebrations were usually homegrown fruits and vegetables used to decorate the dining table or sideboard. It was not until the early part of the twentieth century that manufactured decorations became widely available for the average homemaker.

In 1893 in Cleveland, Ohio, the F.A. Dowling Silver Co. patented a sterling silver spoon bearing an embossed turkey at the top of the handle with an overflowing cornucopia at the center. This pattern was later made in fork form as well.

Since turkeys were in abundant supply during the first holiday celebration, many late nineteenth- and early twentieth-century candy containers were made to commemorate this form. Most are full figure, have separate heads, metal legs, and blown glass eyes. Full-figure chicken and pigeon designs were also common candy containers. Early twentieth-century embossed and lithographed paper and cardboard turkey table decorations often had folded honeycomb tissue paper tails which expanded when opened. A great assortment of full-figure hollow and solid chocolate turkeys were made from German pewter and tin candy molds. Other symbols of the bountiful harvest, made in flat and embossed cardboard to decorate the home and table, included sheaves of wheat, ears of corn, pumpkins, cranberries, apples, and nuts, with the wild turkey most commonly used as the centerpiece.

Wax candles were molded in chicken, turkey, pumpkin, and other gourdlike forms. Miniature Pilgrim boys and girls were also made in candle form. Cardboard cornucopia, or horns of plenty, with embossed decorations were filled with candy and nuts for individual place settings. In the 1940s, some of these cornucopias were made in Japan of woven reeds decorated with plastic or composition fruits and vegetables. Individual nut cups, made with crepe paper decoration, were filled with orange and yellow candy corn. Some were decorated with brilliantly

Group of early 20th-century Thanksgiving decorations including homemade banner, turkey cardboard candy container, candles, and fabric turkeys. PRIVATE COLLECTION.

colored autumn leaves, often with name tags. The five-and-ten-cents store featured molded full-figure glass containers in the shape of turkeys filled with candy.

Again during the early part of this century, paper companies like Dennison manufactured tableware, all having repeating and matching patterns, including plates, napkins, and cups decorated for use at home. Paper cloths for the party and bridge table printed with autumn leaves, flowers such as chrysanthemums, turkeys, fruits, vegetables, cornucopias, and Pilgrim characters were produced.

Dennison issued party magazines and booklets, similar to those for Halloween, with instructions for decorating the home inside and out. Sheaves of wheat and corn stalks with Indian corn and pumpkins were arranged at doorways to signal the arrival of the harvest season and the holiday. These same publications presented table settings, recipes, games, and costumes to augment the festivities. Directions were offered for making cornucopia centerpieces created from a wire form decorated with crepe paper and then filled with fresh fruits and vegetables. Another centerpiece suggestion was to wrap candy wafers in cellophane to form a Pilgrim figure with a handpainted face. Pilgrim dolls, often representing Priscilla in gray and John Alden in somber brown, were made from crepe paper over wire forms and used as party favors, game prizes or centerpieces. A number of magazines carried instructions for fashioning an old-fashioned rocking cradle composed of cardboard filled with bonbons to be used as a party favor or a place card. It was also suggested that Pilgrim dolls be mounted on a cardboard box lid covered with crushed silver paper made to represent Plymouth Rock. Honeycomb tissue paper garlands or bunches of red berries and leafy branches decorated window ledges, tops of windows, mantelpieces, doorways, and door frames.

In the first quarter of the twentieth century, homemade and manufactured banners of cloth and paper for both inside and outside the home proclaimed the day as one for giving thanks for the abundance of the harvest. These swags provided a festive decor for the home. Pilgrim and Indian costumes from the early and middle part of this century used for grade school or historical societies' productions can still be found. Embossed cardboard postal and greeting cards with turkeys (some with feather decorations) and depictions of grandmother's house with hold-to-light windows are extremely collectible.

Thanksgiving Listings

Banner, cotton with embroidered "Happy Thanksgiving," early 20th century, poor condition. $50
Book, party, *Thanksgiving*, Dennison, 1930. .... $10
Books, lot, Dennison party books, Thanksgiving ideas, mid-20th century, stained condition. $10/lot
Bridge tallies, set, turkeys, cut-out, paper with tassels. $5/set
Candle, wax, figural turkey, mid-20th century. $10
Candle, wax, figural, Pilgrim boys and girls, boxed set of six. $75/box
Candy container, chicken, papier-mâché, early 20th century, German, opens on bottom. $125
Candy container, duck, papier-mâché with fabric feet, 1900. .... $275
Candy container, pigeon, papier-mâché, early 20th century, metal legs and feet. $200
Candy container, roast turkey form, papier-mâché, Germany, 5 inches. ... $50
Candy container, turkey, chalk type, metal feet, Germany. $25
Candy container, turkey, composition, bottom closure, Germany, 3½ inches. $45
Candy container, turkey, composition, lead feet, early 20th century. $25
Candy container, turkey, orange-colored cardboard, 1930, opens at bottom. $35
Candy container, turkey, papier-mâché, early 20th century. $150
Candy container, turkey, papier-mâché, full figure, large size, multicolored. $25
Candy container, turkey, papier-mâché, green, black, red, feathers, 4½ inches. $20
Candy container, turkey, papier-mâché, nodder, German, 1920s. $275
Card, greeting, family around Thanksgiving table, mid-20th century. $3
Card, greeting, turkey with feather tail, 1930s. $8
Card, greeting, turkey, "Happy Thanksgiving," mid-20th century. $5
Card, trade, Acme Stove Co., Thanksgiving greetings, embossed cardboard, 1936. .... $7

Card, trade, Singer Sewing Machine, "Happy Thanksgiving," embossed fruit and leaves, 1930. ....$5

Centerpiece, cornucopia, crepe paper over wire frame, 1940. ....$50

Centerpiece, horn of plenty, papier-mâché with paper fruit and nuts, gilt decoration. $35

Centerpiece, table, Indian tepee, crepe paper-covered cardboard on cardboard base, 1930. ....$35

Centerpiece, table, Priscilla and John figures, cardboard with tissue fold-outs, lithographed cardboard base, 1940. ....$55

Centerpiece, turkey, cardboard with honeycomb tissue paper with fold-out tail, 1940. ....$45

Centerpiece, turkey, honeycomb tissue with cardboard base. $25

Centerpiece, turkey, pressed cardboard, orange colored. $35

Centerpiece, turkeys, cardboard with fold-out tissue tails, original box of four. $35/box

Cookie cutter, leaves, turkeys, human figures, set of 12, plastic, mid-20th century. $10/set

Cookie cutter, turkey, aluminum, 1950. ....$5

Cookie cutter, turkey, tin with backplate, early 20th century. $10

Costume, Indian with feather headdress, homemade school costume, 1940. ....$22

Costume, Pilgrim, boy, 1940s, homemade. $15

Decoration, crepe paper printed with border of leaves and fruit, Dennison, original cellophane package, 1930. ....$10

Decoration, streamers, printed crepe paper, turkeys and Pilgrims, 1940, original package. $7

Doorstop, turkey, painted cast iron, early 20th century. $950

Favor, candy box, figures Priscilla and John Alden, lithographed paper. $5

Favor, turkey, composition, painted decoration, 1940s. $5

Invitations, cornucopia, printed cardboard, package. $5

Invitations, Thanksgiving Dinner, handpainted cornucopia, package. $10

Invitations, turkeys, printed cardboard, package. $5

Labels, turkeys, die cut, gummed back, package, early 20th century. ..$7/pkg

Magazine, *Dennison's Party Book*, 1930. ....$15

Menu, Thanksgiving dinner, Hotel Astor, early 20th century. $10

Mold, butter, sheaf of wheat, wooden, early 20th century. $125

Mold, chocolate, cornucopia, early 20th century, tin. $45

Mold, chocolate, ear of corn, tin, early 20th century. $50

Mold, chocolate, turkey, German, 8 inches high. $30

Mold, chocolate, turkey, hinged, tin, Germany, 7½ inches high. $60

Mold, chocolate, turkey, tin, late 19th century, German. $75

Mold, corn stick, iron, early 20th century, miniature size. $45

Mold, ice cream, cornucopia, iron, two-part, circa 1900. ....$75

Mold, ice cream, cornucopia, pewter, early 20th century. $22

Mold, ice cream, cornucopia, pewter, hinged, early 20th century. $20

Mold, ice cream, turkey, pewter, early 20th century, 5 inches. $20

Mold, Jell-O, Pilgrim children, aluminum, mid-20th century. $10

Mold, maple sugar, multiple turkeys, carved wood, early 20th century. $25

Mold, roast turkey, tin, late 19th century, German. $75

Mold, turkey motif, pudding, English, 1930s. $35

Mold, turkey, aluminum, mid-20th century. $10

Napkin, printed paper, Pilgrims and Indians, 1940s, cellophane package. ...$5

Napkin ring, figural, pumpkin, vine, silverplated, late 19th century. $35

Nut basket, cornucopia-shape cardboard, crepe paper frill. $7
Nut basket, woven-straw cornucopia, with name tag, 1930. .... $10
Nut basket, crepe paper with cardboard turkey cut-out. $5
Nut basket, crepe paper, cut-out autumn leaves. $5
Nut cup, canoe, birch bark, homemade with name tag. $10
Nut cup, crepe paper, cardboard, lithographed turkey, name tag. $7
Nut cup, double crepe paper frill, Pilgrim cut-out. $5
Nut cup, woven paper basket, pumpkin decoration. $5
Photograph, Landing of the Pilgrims, grade-school play, 1940. .... $15
Place card, Indian and Pilgrim, lithographed with name tag. $3
Place card, turkey, cardboard cut-out, name tag. $3
Plate, glass, turkey, embossed, 9-inch diameter. $35
Platter, turkey and sheaves of wheat, transfer decoration on pottery, English, 1920. .... $75
Platter, turkey, embossed ironstone pottery, English, early 20th century. .$125
Postcard, boy and girl carrying pumpkin, early 20th century. $5
Postcard, child in Indian headdress chasing turkey, embossed cardboard, early 20th century, German. $5
Postcard, children carrying cornucopia, embossed, 1930. .... $10
Postcard, children with turkeys, embossed cardboard, early 20th century, American. $5
Postcard, couple seated at Thanksgiving dinner table, embossed cardboard, German, early 20th century. $5
Postcard, hold-to-light with grandmother's house. $25
Postcard, leather, "Happy Thanksgiving," early 20th century. $15
Postcard, turkey and pumpkin, printed cardboard, fair condition. $3
Print, Currier and Ives, Landing of the Pilgrims, 13 inches × 17 inches. . $85
Salt and pepper, ears of corn, pottery, early 20th century. $25/pr
Salt and pepper, turkeys, brown and red pottery, mid-20th century. $10/pr
Sheet music, "Turkey Trot," 1930. .... $10
Spoon, Landing of the Pilgrims, sterling silver, early 20th century. $15
Tablecloth, cotton with stenciled turkey, swags of fruit, stained condition, homemade. $10
Tablecloth, linen with embroidered fruit, nuts, and leaves with 12 matching napkins, fine condition. $75/all
Tablecloth, printed paper, Pilgrims and Indians at feast, with matching napkins. $25/set
Tablecloth, printed paper, turkeys and autumn leaves, original package. $5
Table decoration, crepe paper over wire frame dolls, Priscilla and John, circa 1940. ....$25/2
Textile, apron, full, printed fabric, "Happy Thanksgiving," leaf border. $5
Textile, apron, half, organdy with cut-out fabric leaves and berries, circa 1930. .... $12
Tray, turkey motif, spun aluminum, cut-out handles, mid-20th century. ... $20
Wall decoration, cornucopia with fruit, lithographed cardboard, 1940s. ... $10
Wall decoration, pressed cardboard, sheaf of wheat, ears of corn, pumpkins, cranberries. $15

Chanukah

Chanukah, celebrated in mid-winter by the Jewish people, usually in December, is an eight-day celebration begun in Syria at the time of the Maccabees. To purify the Temple sanctuary and to rejoice in their victory when the Maccabees drove the Syrians from the Temple, the Maccabean people found just enough oil left in the Temple coffer to burn for one night. They lit the oil in a Menorah, a nine-branched candelabra; miraculously, the oil burned for eight days and nights. The people rejoiced and established a holiday to commemorate this event.

Chanukah continues today with the lighting of the Menorah. One candle or oil cup is lighted each day with the ninth candle being used as the Shammes, the servant or helper. Menorahs are lit in the synagogue, the house of worship, as well as the home. Many families have Menorahs for each family member. Menorahs, with their flickering candles, are generally placed on the windowsills of the home for all passersby to see. After the holiday and throughout the year, Menorahs are often placed on ledges or shelves for display. They are made from a large variety of materials including sterling silver, brass, copper, pewter, iron, pottery, and glass, and sometimes in combinations of these materials. Lighting receptacles hold either candles or oil. Decorative features include foliage, fruit, cherubs, monsters, Lions of Judah, family crests, birds, trees with spreading branches, scrolls and shell work, eagles, crowns or griffins. Also used is the Star of David, the word Chanukah in Hebrew, or a hand with a jug (containing oil) emerging from a cloud meant to signify the miracle of the length of the burning oil.

Blessings are recited; candles are lit; songs are sung; gifts are exchanged, one for every night of the holiday; and games are played. One of the most popular holiday games is called Spin the Dreidel. Played with a dreidel, a four-sided spinning top, the participants in this gambling game pit their abilities to spin the dreidel against their competitors. The four-sided top, usually made from carved wood, cast pewter, sterling silver or silverplate, is inscribed on each side with Hebrew letters signifying what each player must do with the gelt or money, candy or other food that he or she is using for barter. The letter "Shin" means the player must put money in the kitty. "Nun" indicates the win of nothing; if "Gimel" is your lot, you have won the entire pot; and a spin of "Hay" shows that you win half the pot.

Chanukah Listings

Banner, Chanukah greetings and Menorahs, printed paper, early 20th century. $25
Candy container, cardboard embossed with Menorah, early 20th century. $10
Candy container, flocked cardboard box with cut-out cardboard Star of David, homemade, early 20th century. $25
Card, handpainted, children lighting Menorah, early 20th century, homemade. $15
Cards, Chanukah greetings, embossed paper with gilding, box, mid-20th century. $10/box
Cookie cutter, Menorah, plastic, mid-20th century. $5
Cookie cutter, Star of David, tin, early 20th century. $10
Dreidel, hard plastic, multicolored, mid-20th century. $7
Dreidel, sterling silver, embossed motifs, reproduction. $350
Dreidel, wooden carved Chanukah symbols, early 20th century. $25
Favor, foil-covered coins in net bag, circa 1940, Barricini Chocolate. $7
Garland, foil-covered cardboard, cut-out dreidels, 15-foot length, mid-20th century. $10
Gift paper, gold Star of David on blue ground, mid-20th century. $5
Invitation, Latke Party, Chanukah, 1950. .... $3
Invitation, Menorah in silhouette, cut cardboard, package, early 20th century. $10/pkg
Lamp, Bezalel, small, silver, backplate depicting the Hasmoneans rekindling the Temple Menorah, relevant Hebrew inscriptions along upper edge; fronted by eight removable oil pans in fitted platform; lacking servant light. $1,600
Lamp, Continental, brass, backplate embossed with Star of David, "Chanukah" in Hebrew and other designs, eight oil receptacles, central removable servant light. $325

Left, *Bezalel silver Chanukah lamp, $1,600.* COURTESY OF SWANN GALLERIES.
Right, *mid-19th-century Continental silver Chanukah lamp.* COURTESY OF
PHILLIPS. LONDON.

Left, *early 20th-century pressed tin Chanukah lamp;* right, *mid-20th-century Ludwig Wolpert silver and lucite Chanukah lamp.* PRIVATE COLLECTION.

Lamp, German, silver, the tapering cylindrical stem set on a domed circular base embossed and chased with flower clusters, the tendril stems applied with grape leaves and clusters, each with a baluster candle holder, the center affixed with a matching servant light below an eagle-form knop. $950

Lamp, North African, brass, backplate pierced with elaborate geometric design around central shield above a row of Mirhabs, Star of David at top, front platform with eight oil pans, side panels similarly pierced and crowned with Stars of David. $500

Lamps, pair, American, brass, baluster stem on domed circular base, row of eight candle sockets at top, supported by stylistically curved arms with servant. $425/pr

Menorah, embossed brass Lion of Judah, late 19th century. $200

Menorah, Portuguese, sterling silver, double-domed base, band of rosebuds and foliage on talon feet, branches supporting circular wax pans and urn form sockets with cast and engraved eagle finial and detachable oil pitcher, 21½ inches high. $1,000

Menorah, pressed tin, early 20th century. $85

Streamer, crepe paper, blue and gold, printed "Happy Chanukah," roll, mid-20th century. $5

Tablecloth, cotton with handpainted Menorah and stars, early 20th century, stained condition. $15

Tablecloth, Menorah and dreidel border, printed paper, mid-20th century. ..$5

Christmas

The revered observance of Christmas on December 25, the birth date of Jesus Christ, has evolved into a worldwide religious celebration of peace and joy.

Ornaments and decorations for this holiday, however, are not only religious in content. National, regional, and seasonal influences have dictated the styles and types of holiday decorations. Folk traditions have added to the charisma of the holiday and its observances. All of these have contributed to an overwhelming abundance of items for the collector, both novice and advanced. Lovingly preserved in attics and storerooms, waiting to be placed on the tree, the mantelpiece or the window ledge, treasured decorations have been handed down from generation to generation.

The Santa Claus figure, probably the best loved of all the Christmas symbols, has been known in many countries through the years by various names. In the fourth century, Saint Nicholas, the Bishop of Myra, became known for his gift giving. Upon his death, his good works were remembered and people continued to commemorate the date of his birth by presenting gifts, especially to children. During the Middle Ages, the birth of Christ was celebrated with parties and the exchanging of gifts of gold and jewels among the noblemen and their ladies. But, in the sixteenth century during the Protestant Reformation, it became unpopular to celebrate a holiday in honor of a saint. To continue an already time-honored and extremely popular observance, the figure of Saint Nicholas had to evolve into Father Christmas to survive. He appeared in illustrations during that period as a thin stern figure wearing robes trimmed with fur, having his head crowned with a wreath of holly or mistletoe. He sometimes carried a yule log, several switches (for children who misbehaved) or a bag of toys. In England, he was known as Father Christmas, and in France, Pere Noel.

During the eighteenth century, the idea of Kris Kringle was brought to America by the Germans who settled in Pennsylvania. Over the years, through transplanting from one culture to another, continued usage, and corruption of the languages, the German symbol of the Christ Child, known as Christkind, became Kris Kringle, another name for Santa Claus. All of these various names have led to much confusion regarding

Two early 20th-century Belsnickles with fur beards. COURTESY OF SKINNER AUCTIONS.

the man and who accompanied him on his appointed rounds of gift giving. During the 1800s, sinister representations of Saint Nicholas, sometimes thought to accompany the Christ Child, evolved from the name Pelz Nicol to Belsnickle. Today some believe that the Santa character was accompanied by a Belsnickle or Krampus figure, an evil-looking man, who followed Saint Nicholas and gave switches rather than toys or other goodies to bad boys and girls. At the same time, the Dutch knew this person as Sinter Cloes, which also, in translation, was Anglicized and evolved into Santa Claus.

The complete transformation and solid identity of Santa Claus was established in the United States by the middle of the nineteenth century. In 1822, Doctor Clement Clarke Moore wrote his famous poem, *A Visit From Saint Nicholas*, for his own six children:

His eyes—how they twinkled! His dimples—how merry!
His cheeks were like roses, his nose like a cherry!
His droll like mouth was drawn up like a bow,
And the beard on his chin was as white as the snow. . . .
He had a broad face and a little round belly
That shook, when he laughed, like a bowl full of jelly.
He was chubby and plump, a right jolly old elf.

Early 19th-century Schnerenschnitte valentine mounted on paper. PHOTO COURTESY OF NANCY ROSIN.

Mid–19th-century hand-painted and embossed paper lace valentine. PHOTO COURTESY OF NANCY ROSIN.

Late 19th-century vinegar valentines. PHOTO COURTESY OF NANCY ROSIN.

Valentine, circa 1900, embossed card-board. PHOTO COURTESY OF NANCY ROSIN.

Early 20th-century lithographed paper and honeycomb tissue valentine. PHOTO COURTESY OF NANCY ROSIN.

Early 20th-century lithographed paper and honeycomb tissue valentine. PHOTO COURTESY OF NANCY ROSIN.

Early 20th-century lithographed paper valentine with googly eyed children. PHOTO COURTESY OF NANCY ROSIN.

Early 20th-century lithographed Easter pull toy with rabbit candy container. PHOTO COURTESY OF JOAN AND ALLAN LEHNER.

Group of early 20th-century lithographed paper over cardboard Easter egg candy containers. PHOTO COURTESY OF JOAN AND ALLAN LEHNER.

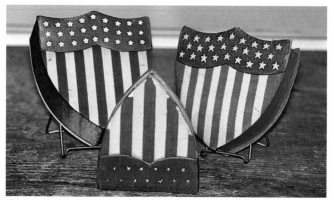

Group of late 19th-century candy containers used for Fourth of July. PHOTO COURTESY OF JOAN AND ALLAN LEHNER.

Group of early 20th-century Halloween decorations. Top shelf: glass lanterns with painted decoration. Second shelf: candy containers. Third shelf: combination of both. PHOTO COURTESY OF JOAN AND ALLAN LEHNER.

Early 20th-century Halloween roly-poly candy containers. PHOTO COURTESY OF JOAN AND ALLAN LEHNER.

Early 20th-century Halloween lanterns. PHOTO COURTESY OF JOAN AND ALLAN LEHNER.

Father Christmas candy container, late 19th century. PHOTO COURTESY OF JOAN AND ALLAN LEHNER.

Christmas puzzle, circa 1900. PHOTO COURTESY OF JOAN AND ALLAN LEHNER.

Santa figures, left to right: candle holder, bottles, and lantern. PHOTO
COURTESY OF JOAN AND ALLAN LEHNER.

Santa figure candy container, circa 1900. PHOTO
COURTESY OF JOAN AND ALLAN LEHNER.

Santa figure with mica flakes, early 20th century. PHOTO COURTESY OF JOAN AND ALLAN LEHNER.

Left to right: early 20th-century miniature tree with gifts, feather tree, and candy container with village scene on lid. PRIVATE COLLECTION.

Thomas Nast, political cartoonist renowned for his satirical characterizations, originally sketched Santa for *Harper's Weekly* magazine in 1863. The following year he portrayed Santa wearing stars and stripes presenting gifts to Union soldiers. Both men were among the first to portray Santa as a plump jolly gentleman in a red suit with white fur trim. It was certainly easier for the public to accept the Santa figure as a jolly old man rather than a harsh curmudgeon to usher in the joyous spirit of Christmas.

Following the Civil War, the United States enjoyed a period of prosperity with worldly goods in plentiful supply. Extravagantly elaborate Christmas celebrations, commonly held by many families, led to excesses in gifts, food stuffs, and decorations. People enjoyed and decorated Christmas trees. Both city and country families had access to more and different varieties of store-bought decorations in addition to those made at home. The exuberance of the late Victorian period is exemplified in the variety and abundance of homemade decorations and gifts. Socializing in the afternoons, women gathered at one another's homes to embroider bibs, aprons, gentlemen's suspenders, and handkerchiefs for Christmas gifts. Children were taught to make pen wipes, bookmarks, stuffed dolls, carved wooden whistles, and paper chains for the tree. In response to demand, ladies' magazines of the period explained how to make ornaments, decorations, gifts, and baked goods for the holidays. Exchanging handmade and commercially colored Christmas and postal cards also became popular.

During the late nineteenth and early part of the twentieth centuries, Santa figures, used to decorate the mantel or window ledge either in the form of the thin austere Father Christmas or the plump jolly variety, were usually composition and wore either fur or velvet suits. Red is common but the colors green, white, and blue were also used for the costume. Ranging in size from about 2 inches to several feet in height, these Santas were used for table, mantel or tree decorations. Occasionally the figures held yule logs, small Christmas trees, switches or a bundle of switches, and were enhanced with traces of glitter.

At the turn of the twentieth century in Lauscha, Germany, a cottage industry developed making figures from cotton batting. This material was called cotton wool in Europe and England. Die cut, embossed pictures were used for faces and hands. At times the workers used a dried bog heather to simulate greenery on their creations. Sometimes Father Christmas figures were made with papier-mâché or had bisque faces and hands. Occasionally they carried feather trees in addition to other greens. The feather tree could also be carried alone. Most of the figures were set on wooden bases, with the rarest having nodding heads. Also at this time, machines were developed to wrap spun glass around forms in the shape of Father Christmas, which were then supplied with handpainted wax heads. These are extremely rare in today's marketplace.

Some Santa figures were used as table centerpieces; others held packs on their backs for candy and other sweets (these are not considered true candy containers). The smallest figures were made to hang on trees or to be used for package decorations. By the late nineteenth century, celluloid was also used to mold the Father Christmas figure. In addition, both Father Christmas and Santa figures were made in wood; and at the same time, they were also made in lead so that they were similar to toy soldiers. Tin and cast-iron figures were sometimes in the form of banks. Rare examples were made in chalk with brightly colored decoration. A chalk church is also known to exist and may have been part of a village scene used under the tree.

At the turn of the twentieth century, particularly in the United States, lithographed tin was used for making toys depicting Santa Claus. These were sold through mail-order catalogs, toy stores, and five-and-dime stores like Woolworth's. Solid and hollow chocolate formed in tin molds depicted Saint Nicholas, Father Christmas, and Santa Claus, varying in size from a few inches to several feet in height. The molds were made in Germany at the end of the nineteenth and the beginning of the twentieth centuries. Different versions were available, some with trees, others with an individual or a sackful of toys. All over the world, beginning in the late nineteenth century, carved wooden molds, very often in the shape of Kris Kringle or Santa Claus, were made for gingerbread and other types of cookies. The cookies were frosted with handpainted colors or decorated with die cut pictures depicting Santa Claus. Many of these cookies were used for tree decorations.

Left, *early 20th-century Father Christmas holding feather tree;* right, *early 20th-century Dutch St. Nicholas figure, composition face, $495.*
COURTESY OF TERRY AND JOE DZIADUL.

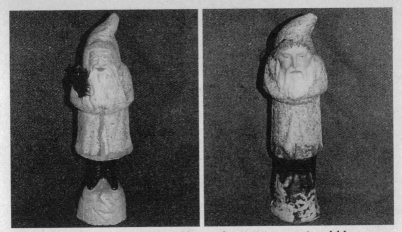

Left, *early 20th-century Belsnickle candy container, painted blue lapels, $675;* right, *early 20th-century Belsnickle candy container, white robe with mica decoration, $495.* COURTESY OF TERRY AND JOE DZIADUL.

At the turn of the twentieth century, papier-mâché Santa figures holding tinsel, holly, candles or in combination with a sleigh and reindeer, often in pressed cardboard or papier-mâché, were also used for table, window or mantel decorations. These became extraordinarily fashionable for decorating tables at children's parties. At this same time, Germany manufactured molded, full-figure, papier-mâché candle holders in the form of the head of Father Christmas with a flat bottom for use on a table, at a window or with a wire to hang from the tree. These are extremely rare today. Early twentieth-century German doll makers, known for the fine quality of their products, began to make bisque heads and hands for use on Father Christmas and Santa Claus figures. At the same time, these were copied in Japan where the ceramic faces tended to be rougher and have gritty sandlike appearances. After World War I, Japan expanded production of toys and holiday decorations to meet the public's demand and became the world's largest exporter of these wares. Most of the Japanese figures had cotton beards and were dressed in suits of chenille, crepe paper or flannel and carried bottle-brush trees, whereas the German figures carried goose-feather trees. Red and green chenille bells in graduated sizes were also produced with handpainted celluloid or bisque faces depicting Santa and having chenille roping and loops.

Candy containers made by the Japanese depicted Santas with celluloid faces, often garishly painted, and sometimes carrying toys in a sack of netting. The German Santa candy containers generally had lithographed die cuts for the faces. Early twentieth century Santas and sleds were made in both Germany and Japan. The German sled were almost always wood; the Japanese versions were cardboard with celluloid reindeer.

Late 19th-century cornucopia candy containers.

COURTESY OF JOAN AND ALLAN LEHNER.

Some candy containers depicting Santa were made for hanging on the tree. Others were made as decorations for the table or mantelpiece. A quantity were homemade from instruction pages found in early twentieth-century monthly ladies' magazines. Full-figure candy containers depicting Belsnickles and Santas became popular at the turn of the twentieth century. Many German examples were made in two parts so that they could be filled with homemade candies. On most types, the head lifts off the figure. Others have joints at the center (waist) or the base can be removed for filling. There are also very fine examples in which Santa was made sitting on a felt-covered cardboard reindeer or horse, complete with leather bridle, or on a sled. The figure could be easily removed to fill the body of the animal or the sled with candy. Japanese candy containers from the 1930s were generally constructed from cardboard, sometimes with celluloid faces. Often they portrayed Santa on top of a chimney, in a bright red Christmas boot or in a pressed board sled with mica trim. In the late nineteenth and early part of the twentieth centuries when various modes of transportation became popular, Santas were depicted in moss-covered bicycles, tricycles, zeppelins, hot air balloons or seated in straw, wood, celluloid, rubber or cardboard automobiles or airplanes.

The outdoor use of Christmas trees, a pagan tradition begun by the

Early 20th-century Santa candy container.

COURTESY OF JOAN AND ALLAN LEHNER.

Druids and other early peoples, signaled the return of spring. The tree was brought inside the Roman Catholic church in the Middle Ages. In the 1700s, the sugar tree was decorated to celebrate the holiday. A great many of the sweets were gilded and hung while others were left plain to be eaten from the sugar tree. Decorated by the Germans as early as the seventeenth century, trees were probably brought by them to the United States in the middle part of the eighteenth century. When the Pennsylvania Germans first arrived in this country, they also decorated tabletop trees. At the exact same period, a wooden pyramid-shaped frame was wrapped with evergreen boughs and decorated with candles and cookies. The eighteenth-century tree was usually decorated with small candles, strings of cranberries, popcorn, cookies, and nuts. Shapes of cookies included stars, crescents, farm animals, and human figures. In 1845, the children's book, *Kris Kringle's Christmas Tree*, was published in Philadelphia and showed a Santa figure carrying a tree for the children.

By the latter part of the nineteenth century, tree decorating became widespread throughout the United States and Europe. Decorations encompassed handmade and store-bought ornaments, most often made in Germany. These were in the form of blown glass animals, flowers, fruits, drums, horns, flags, and human figures, commonly in figural shape. Blown glass balls or kugels, glass icicles, and reflectors of shiny cut tin were also made. This period also saw the use of cardboard cornucopias filled with homemade candies or tiny toys, candy containers, and ornaments decorated with embossed paper, paper lace or glitter, and sometimes with all three. Ornaments also included tiny beribboned woven

*Group of
Kugels,
feather trees,
and fences.*
COURTESY OF
GARTH'S AUCTIONS.

Group of late 19th- and early 20th-century blown glass, papier-mâché,

baskets filled with homemade candy or wax dolls with golden human hair and gossamer fabric wings. Trees were hung with toys such as dolls, doll furniture, tiny musical instruments, paint sets, children's jewelry, toy guns, swords, spinning tops, pen wipes, posey holders, and velvet fruit of all kinds. Children created a variety of homemade ornaments including gilded pine cones or walnuts, paper chains, paper roses, and polished apples. By this time trees of ceiling height, often 12 feet tall, were popular. Miniature paper American flags and shield-shaped candy containers in red, white, and blue with stars and stripes were used as tree decorations at the time of the centennial. To heighten the anticipation, trees were usually hidden from the children until Christmas morning. Oftentimes, the tree decorated today for the ballet "The Nutcracker Suite" reflects this style of Victorian tradition.

and Dresden ornaments. COURTESY OF SALLIE AND BOB CONNELLY.

The first artificial trees were the German feather trees introduced in the late eighteenth century. They were extremely popular and began to be commercially produced at the latter part of the nineteenth century. The trees were produced from twigs or wooden dowels wrapped with dyed green goose or turkey feathers which were inserted into a tree trunk or another wooden dowel and then placed into a wooden base. White feather trees were also developed during this time. For our current taste, these feather trees sometimes appear to have a sparse appearance. Tiny feather trees were used with Santa Claus figures in nativity scenes or as table or mantel decorations. These were replaced in the early twentieth century by trees made from wire and bristles, referred to as bottle-brush trees. Commonly used to decorate doll house-style villages or train sets, the trees were made in great quantities in the United States and Japan.

Sometimes covered with artificial snow, hung with blown glass balls or cotton ornaments, they were set on red wooden bases. With the advent of World War I, feather trees were no longer imported from Germany and began to be produced in the United States. These were generally marked "Made in USA." Feather trees, along with green cellophane-wrapped trees, were in use until World War II.

Aluminum or spun glass artificial trees, from tabletop size to seven feet in height, then began to be produced in quantities. They were manufactured in natural color, white, silver or blue, often decorated with tiny bells. Gold or silver satin bows decorated the trees. This was the period for "decorator" trees, a time when it was considered chic to have an all-white tree with silver decorations or an all-silver tree with only blue decorations. Trees were extremely stylized with only candle or glitter decoration. The old-fashioned or homemade look became passé.

The tree itself was a popular motif used in a variety of decorations. Full-figure honeycomb tissue paper trees were made as table centerpieces. Smaller ones became table decorations or were incorporated into cards during the early and middle part of the twentieth century.

Prior to the late nineteenth century when the tree was brought inside, stone jars or wooden tubs filled with sand often held the tree upright. Stylization of Christmas tree stands followed the decorative styles of the furnishings of the period. By the late nineteenth century, cast iron became popular and began to be used for stands. Some of the stands contained receptacles which were able to be filled with water to keep the tree fresh.

Design motifs included scroll work, angels' heads, Santas, tree branches, ferns, and later Arts and Crafts and Art Deco zig-zag motifs, sometimes with painted decoration. At the turn of the twentieth century, musical stands were manufactured in Germany. In the 1920s and '30s, stands with lights began to be used. Concrete stands, sometimes modeled in the form of Santa's head with red, green, and white paint, then made their way into use. It is interesting to note that when these stands were first produced, the average family was unable to afford them because they were so expensive. By the middle part of the twentieth century, red and green plastic stands, sometimes with water reservoirs and revolving mechanisms, became available.

Some people used a sheet or other old fabric to cover the floor under the tree to prevent candle wax from dripping on the floor, to contain the needles from the tree or to serve as a background for the nativity scene. But, by the early part of the twentieth century, the demand for products to finish dressing the tree stimulated the production of commercial tree carpets for an eager public. These were most often painted, with some depicting Santa in a sleigh pulled by reindeer. "Merry Christmas" was sometimes the imprint. Cotton batting was also used, and, most often, by the 1950s the tree carpets were sprinkled with glitter. Known as tree skirts or carpets, directions for making them were in ladies' magazines of the period.

Another complement to the tree was the fence encircling the floor covering, often used to surround the nativity scene. The earliest examples, dating from the latter part of the nineteenth century, were miniature replicas of fencing used for Victorian homes. The first were wooden, handmade in sections, oftentimes with gates. Ranging from 3 to 10 inches in height, commercial examples, again simulating fences from homes of the period, were made in wood, cast iron, and tin, with a number having arched Gothic motifs. Examples in wicker, picket, and post and rail were made. In the 1900s, red and green were popular colors. In 1920, cast-iron posts with electric lights were popular; and, by 1930, goose feather fencing simulating hedges became the rage.

Since almost the beginnings of recorded celebrations for this holiday, it has been common practice to include a nativity or creche scene at the base of one's Christmas tree. Derived from an old German custom also known as the Putz, Christ's birth in the manger in Bethlehem was recorded through full-figure representations depicting Christ, Mary, Joseph, and the Three Wise Men. Animals, such as camels, sheep, cows, donkeys, and horses, were sometimes displayed. Through the years, the stable scene evolved into elaborate village scenes with multiple houses, trees, animals, and human figures constructed of handcarved or machine-made wood, as well as examples in bisque, lithographed tin, cardboard, celluloid, plaster, composition or coated cardboard. Some of the animals, such as lambs, were covered with cloth to simulate fur. Using straw and other natural fibers in the circle under the tree was meant to simulate the tree's natural habitat. From the latter part of the nineteenth century through the 1950s, chromolithographed cardboard boxed sets of the Putz, similar

Early 20th-century creche figures. COURTESY OF JOAN AND ALLAN LEHNER.

to paper doll sets, were sold. In the 1930s, many of the village buildings had mica flakes imitating snow on roof tops. In some versions of these villages, the windows of houses could be electrified and were covered with colored cellophane. Even though reindeer were not in the original nativity, they sometimes were used in the scene. The first examples were made of wood in Germany. Later they were manufactured in cast iron or lead. Celluloid examples were made in Japan. Oftentimes all had painted decoration.

Other decorations for under the tree included snow babies—miniature bisque figures covered with raised pottery flakes to resemble snow, often with handpainted faces. Ranging in size from 1½ inches to 4 inches in height, some skied while others sledded, skated, rode polar bears or tossed snowballs. Occasionally, these figures were made with jointed limbs. The best examples were manufactured in Germany in the 1920s and '30s and had exceptionally fine clarity of features. They were also made in Japan with less attention to details. Miniature colored bisque figures depicting Santa alone or Santa on a sled, chimney or roof top were made in Germany and Japan in the early part of the twentieth century. These, too, were used for decoration under the tree.

Candles, representing Christ as the light of the world, were first used to illuminate Christmas trees in southern Germany in the latter part of the seventeenth century. Despite the constant threat of fires, they were widely used. They were eventually replaced by oil lamps, however, usually miniature in size. Often, since candles were so expensive, half a nut shell with a cord inserted as a wick for the oil was used in place of a candle. By the 1870s when wax candles were widely available for the general public, holders for them became popular. The first styles, most often purchased in sets of 12 in various sizes, were tin holders clipped upright on the tree limb and made with crimped drip pans to catch the

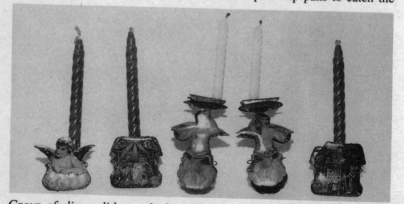

Group of clip-on lithographed candle holders, circa 1890, $125–$150.
COURTESY OF JOE AND TERRY DZIADUL.

wax dripping from the lighted candles. Clips in figural forms featured birds, butterflies, angels or stars, often handpainted in bright colors. Others had embossed decorative patterns depicting angels, Santas, butterflies or children. The most elaborate clip-ons had blown glass candle shades in the form of molded flowers, fruits or children's faces. First patented in the United States in 1867, balance or counterbalance candle holders, made with a tin candle cup and wax pan at the top, a long thin wire in the middle, and a colored clay or lead ball at the base, were also extremely popular. This bottom weight insured that the candle remained upright on the tree. The Germans improved on the counterweight and replaced the balls with figural weights in forms similar to those of the clip-on variety, such as angels, birds, butterflies or stars.

Another way of illuminating the tree was by using tin or brass lanterns, some in figural house or building form, with a small candle having colored mica, gelatin or isinglass windows. At the turn of the twentieth century, celluloid was also used for lanterns. Since, however, this material was highly flammable, few examples have survived.

Tin and lead Christmas ornaments were first made in the latter part of the eighteenth century by toy makers in Nuremburg, Germany, who also produced metal doll dishes and furniture. Most popular in America in the late nineteenth century, these decorations were produced in geometric and animal shapes and in the form of birdcages, baskets or cradles. When these were meant to hang from a tree, they were suspended by string. Figural tin decorations in these forms also served as counterbalance weights for clip-on candle holders. The metal was often brightly painted and could be inset with glass to reflect light and simulate jewels. Tinsel-wrapped wire was used by glass ornament makers to form airplanes, balloons, and boats, as well as alone to twist around flower baskets, sleighs, houses or hot air balloons.

Late 19th-century Santa figure in rattan sleigh with key-wind reindeer nodder with composition antlers, $3,400. COURTESY OF TERRY AND JOE DZIADUL.

Wax Christmas decorations were cast in molds by German toy makers very early in the nineteenth century. The first were miniature replicas of the Baby Jesus. Angels, solid in construction with spun glass or cardboard wings, tinsel or ribbon embellishments, and wire halos, followed and were the most common wax ornament. Later, hollow figures in the form of animals and children were also made. Larger and more elaborate angels appeared in the early part of the twentieth century. Few wax ornaments have survived because they are fragile in nature and respond poorly to fluctuations in temperature.

By the early part of the nineteenth century, glass blowing had become a cottage industry. It was begun about 200 years earlier in the mountain villages of Germany. Blowing a kugel, literally a large hollow ball, created a whimsey. Blown by the father and silvered and handpainted by the wife and children, kugels were often produced in mercury or silvered glass to reflect the candle lights of the tree. What developed as a novelty evolved into a highly successful commercial venture with many saleable items. Demand for kugels, especially those with silver interiors which created a shiny finish, became increasingly intense. Contests developed to see how large one could blow the molten glass. As production increased, molds of wood or plaster had to be created to produce more mold-blown kugels. One can discern the difference by looking for the mold line. The earliest kugels were silvered with lead or zinc instead of silver nitrate or mercury. Free-blown examples are earlier, rarer, and more desirable than later ones. The largest examples are prized. Many were embellished with handpainting and frostings of glitter.

Kugels were produced in a variety of shapes: oval or egg form, round or ball shape. One of the most popular forms is the molded grape. Rarer molded shapes include the pear, turnip, and bell. Most examples, either free-blown or molded, range from 1½ inches to more than 18 inches in diameter. In addition to silver being the most common color, kugels were made in a variety of hues: gold; cobalt and light blue; light and dark green; light red, which is similar to rose; dark red, which is very scarce; and amethyst, the rarest of all colors. Kugels, produced worldwide until after World War II, in addition to being made in Germany, were also produced in Austro-Hungary (part of which changed to Czechoslovakia after World War I), France, and the United States. Smaller versions were used as tree ornaments while larger ones served as house or store decorations. In the middle of the nineteenth century, schecken kugel, meaning those with spotted decoration, were manufactured. The glass maker dipped the blown glass ball into hot wax. If it survived this dip and the sudden change in temperature, the ball developed a crackled appearance. Few of this type of kugel are known.

Blown, molded, figural glass ornaments evolved from the tradition of blowing kugels. At first, glass ornaments were molded into various shapes

Group of glass Christmas ornaments. COURTESY OF BARB AND DICK SHILVOCK.

by blowing bubbles into wooden cookie molds. Specialized molds were then developed expressly for the decorations. One can recognize the earlier glass ornaments by the pike or stem covered with a metal cap used for hanging the ornament from the tree. The pike was broken off after the glass had cooled. Decorating the ornaments was entirely by hand, a continuation of the glass producer's cottage industry. Each ornament was silvered by swishing silver nitrate inside the glass walls. Excess nitrate was removed and reused. Individual ornaments were then hung to dry.

Group of early 20th-century blown glass Christmas ornaments.
COURTESY OF
SKINNER AUCTIONS.

After drying, each ornament was dipped in colored lacquers and then handpainted. By the latter part of the nineteenth century, production included carved, wooden two-part molds in the form of pine cones, fruits and vegetables, horns, drums, houses and buildings, dogs, cats, clowns, the Christ Child in his crib, the fish which represented Christ, birds (especially those native to Germany), angels, Santa Claus figures, hearts with mottoes stating "Merry Christmas" or "Love," parrots, owls, pipes, figures depicting Foxy Grandpa and other comic characters, hot air balloons, and, by the 1920s, cars.

Ornaments were also handblown without molds. By using wooden tools in addition to their glass-blowing skills, the artisans were able to produce teapots with spouts and handles, horns, lyres, and bells. Unsilvered glass ornaments were decorated with soft pastel colors and tinsel or chenille wire. This group included sailboats, swans with long necks, clocks, and birdcages. All species of birds had tails made from spun glass and metal spring legs glued to the bird and then soldered to a clip-on device, used to attach the bird to the tree. Silver and gilt wire, chenille wire, cotton batting, and tinsel were elements often added to individual ornaments for decoration. These ornaments were "best sellers" when they were introduced at Woolworth's and similar variety stores, and in mail-order catalogs of the 1880s such as Sears Roebuck. Woolworth's was the largest importer of blown glass ornaments, and America's insatiable appetite for glass ornaments from the latter part of the nineteenth through the early part of the twentieth centuries was the glass blower's dream come true.

In the 1890s, Czechoslovakian glass bead makers blew hollow glass tubing into beads to form star and circle as well as basket shapes to be used as festoon decorations for the tree. Reflectors and indents, glass ornaments blown in a mold and pressed in at the sides to produce a concave surface with handpainted or silvered finish dusted with glitter, were also made at the same time. Tree toppers or spikes were blown in the form of angels. They were silvered just as the figural ornaments and decorated with spun glass. Stars were also made as tree toppers as well as glass beads in star form. Glass beads with a die cut picture depicting an angel and glass tree tips or points were also made. They ranged in size from 6 to 15 inches.

Wooden toys, created by wood carvers in the mountain areas of Germany during the middle and latter part of the nineteenth century, were also used as tree ornaments. These included handcarved and painted soldiers, swords, bird houses, dolls and doll furniture, whistles, jointed figures, and jumping jacks.

Chromolithographs, also known as die cuts or scraps because the process of cutting the sheets of colorfully decorated printed paper was called die cutting, were made in Germany into Christmas ornaments that be-

Group of blown-glass figural ornaments. PRIVATE COLLECTION.

Blown glass clip-on ornament in shape of pheasant together with clip-on flower candle shade.

BOTH COURTESY OF BARB AND DICK SHILVOCK.

Group of clip-on blown glass bird ornaments. PRIVATE COLLECTION.

Left, *early and mid-20th-century angel tree tops.* PRIVATE COLLECTION.
Right, *early 20th-century Santa jack-in-the-box.* COURTESY OF MARY AND BOB
SCHNEIDER.

*Blown glass icicles, ornaments spun glass and die cut, and Dresden
ornaments.* COURTESY OF SALLIE AND BOB CONNELLY AND SKINNER AUCTIONS.

came popular during the middle of the nineteenth century. Flat sheets of paper were embossed to give a three-dimensional effect, then separated into individual pieces or silhouettes. Most often in the shape of angels, Santa Claus figures, Christmas trees, snow men, children, hearts, flowers, butterflies, stars, animals or musical instruments, they were traded, placed in scrap books, used to decorate Christmas cookies or combined with cotton batting or spun glass for use as tree decorations. Attaching tinsel wire to these forms converted them to hang on the tree. Die cut angels' heads, combined with spun glass skirts, were used as tree toppers or ornaments. Curly strands of spun glass, called angel hair, were draped on the tree for a snowy effect. It was also used to form the hair on figures of angels or small children. Die cuts were added as decoration to plain paper cornucopias, which were then filled with homemade or store-bought candy, and used as candy containers to decorate the tree.

Making decorations by combining cotton batting and scraps began as a cottage industy in Germany in the latter part of the nineteenth century. Die cut Santa or angel heads were added to thin layers of cotton batting to form a body. They were folded, glued over a wire frame, and often sprinkled with glitter. In the twentieth century, examples were also made at home.

In the late nineteenth century, cotton batting was twisted and pressed into a mold to form ornaments in figural fruit and vegetable shapes to hang on the tree. Glue was used to solidify the shape. Then the piece was handtinted or painted, and occasionally sprinkled with mica flakes.

Left, *late 19th-century cotton batting Father Christmas on cardboard base with die cut face, $325.* COURTESY OF TERRY AND JOE DZIADUL. Right, *turn-of-the-20th-century batting ornaments with die cut decorations.*
COURTESY OF JOAN AND ALLAN LEHNER.

Figures included human and animal forms, musical instruments, dolls, balls, and eggs. By the mid-1920s, the Japanese sold pressed cotton ornaments to American consumers. These ornaments were in the shape of Santas, skiers, and human figures with bisque faces, which were brightly painted pink. Since the cotton on these figures was not wrapped as tightly as that on the figures made in Germany, it was softer in appearance. Most of these Japanese figures date between World War I and II. A few are marked "Made in Occupied Japan."

Late nineteenth century glass icicles were first free blown and later mold blown. Clear at first, they were then made in blue, green, and amber with glass loops for hanging. Some of the clear glass examples were silvered. They were replaced by silver metal icicles in the 1930s and strands twisted with color soon thereafter.

First used in the 1870s, tinsel, draped on the Christmas tree in combination with glass ornaments, reflected light in an era when there were no electric lights. Made in strips from a combination of wire and foil which was snipped to produce the crinkled strands, tinsel was sold in varying lengths to decorate the tree with garlands. Foil wrapped over cardboard was used for making decorations during the same period. Foil was also used to make dresses for angels or cut into geometric forms to be used as light reflectors or ornaments, cornucopia or candy containers in the form of Santa's boot. Star-shaped tree tops were also produced. In Germany in 1878, strips of foil, known as Lametta, were cut into smaller lengths and hung on the tree as icicles. These strips were manufactured in gold or silver and tarnished easily. By 1920 in America, icicles were made from lead. In the 1960s, however, the danger from lead poisoning caused this style to be replaced with silver mylar strips.

As early as the 1870s, celluloid ornaments were created in Germany. This highly flammable material, molded into the shape of birds, reindeer, Santas, and birdcages, caused many tree fires. In the early 1920s, the Japanese produced full-figure animals and other stylized figures with a celluloid ring attached to the body. Without the ring, the object is classified as a creche figure, not a tree ornament.

Dresdens, the most desirable and collectible of Christmas ornaments, were produced by several companies in the town from which they derived their name in Germany at the turn of the twentieth century until about the time of the first World War. These decorations are among the rarest because they were handmade. Cardboard figures, 2 to 3 inches in height, were double sided, embossed, and die cut, usually in gold or silver, and then handpainted. Shapes included a large variety of fish, bears, eagles, peacocks, sun faces, moon and stars, angels, skates, zeppelins, boats, bicycles, horns, harps, guitars, doll carriages, coronation coaches, and sleds. Often constructed with very intricate detailing, gold and silver foil, chenille wire, ribbons, and cotton batting added embellishment to create a three-dimensional effect. A loop of string or thread was attached to each whereby they were able to hang on the tree. Originally these decorations were not as popular here as they were in Europe.

Chenille, a fabric-covered wire used most often in Japan to make ornaments, became popular in the early twentieth century. They were manufactured in a variety of forms. Candy canes ranged in size from 2 to 12 inches in length. Santas with scrap or bisque faces and wreaths with foil-covered candle centers were produced. Bells, either all chenille or chenille with bisque or celluloid faces and often in graduated sizes, roping, and stars wrapped with chenille were additional choices used to decorate the tree or home. There were also individual bell-shaped cardboard candy containers with bottom openings covered in chenille roping complete with loops for hanging on the tree.

During the early part of the twentieth century, figural lanterns were also produced in a variety of forms not normally associated with Christmas including a witch, a devil, and an aviator. Pressed glass fairy lights, suspended from branches of the tree and each filled with a wick and oil, were made in the late nineteenth century in many patterns including hob nail, daisy and button, crosshatch, and thousand eye. They were also made in a variety of colors: amber, amethyst, green, cobalt, ruby, and milk glass. At the same time in Germany, glass makers blew their own versions of these types of tree lights which had flowers, beehives, and flowers with human faces, some with handpainted decoration. Fire was an ever-present hazard with all of these ways of lighting the tree. Many a tree with its beautiful flickering lights was consumed in flames. Candle lights, popular until the 1920s when electricity gained widespread use, were then relegated to attic storage or the garbage heap. Using electricity for decorating the Christmas tree was cleaner and easier. In addition, the tree was able to be left unattended. Electricity was new and newest was always best in the mind of the average American consumer.

The widespread use of electricity saw lamps replace candles in most homes as Christmas decorations. Figural glass lamps and shades in the form of Santa, Santa atop a chimney, and Father Christmas holding a tree were manufactured. Cast-iron wreaths with an electric candle center

Late 19th-century pressed glass Christmas lights, $25–$35 each. COURTESY OF MARGARET SCOTT CARTER.

were made for use at a window. Full-figure, colorful Santa light bulbs were also made as window or mantel decorations. Bubble lights, marketed in 1946 immediately following World War II by Noma, contained a chemical inside the tube. When combined with the heat of the electricity, the liquid boiled and the light began to "bubble." At the same time, strings of bulbs, some with bubble lights, in the form of candles were produced. These gave the appearance of a lit taper without the messy dripping of the wax. Following World War II, chenille wreaths with electrified candles in the center were popular window decorations. Plastic replaced glass figural Santa lamps. Those with an interior light bulb were popular in the 1950s.

Early twentieth century electric Christmas lights were sold in strings or festoons and cost as much as a man's weekly salary. Mazda, a division of General Electric and a prominent light bulb manufacturer at this time, made miniature lights for the trees. At first the shapes resembled miniature light bulbs. Later they were changed to a ball and then a cone form. Before World War I, figural bulbs were produced and then hand-painted in Austria. Light in weight and made from transparent glass, the ornaments were produced in the shape of fruits, flowers, animals, clowns, snow men, Santa Claus, and other human figures. In addition to the traditional Christmas characters, other styles, such as witches and jack-o'-lanterns, became popular and were manufactured not as Halloween decorations but for the Christmas tree. Later these were also made in Germany, Japan, and the United States. Japan made thicker and cruder glass versions of the Austrian bulbs. When the Japanese were imitating the Austrian bulbs in the 1920s, they were made in milk glass with poor-quality paint which easily chipped so that cracks showed through when the bulb was plugged in. Prior to 1940, Japan was the major exporter of light bulbs with Christmas motifs. They also made figural bulbs in Dick Tracy, Popeye, and Santa Claus forms, all having slightly Oriental facial features. Strings of Disney characters, using a regular bulb with a plastic shade decorated with a Disney decal, were introduced in the United States at the 1939 World's Fair by the Noma Co. In 1925, 15 small light bulb manufacturing companies had merged to form the National Outfit Manufacturer's Association or NOMA.

Heavy glass ornaments began to be produced in Brooklyn, New York, by the Double Glo Co. in the first quarter of the twentieth century. Their inventory encompassed such Disney characters as Snow White and the Seven Dwarfs. In the 1930s, the Corning Glass Co. in Corning, New York, machine produced Christmas tree balls, primarily for Woolworth's. The ornaments, most often silver painted and brightly color decorated, were later manufactured under the name Shiny Brite. During World War II, there was a scarcity of colorings available for decorating the ornaments; they were made in clear glass, therefore, with a very light striping of color. Shiny Brite developed into the largest producer of ornaments in the world.

Red honeycomb tissue paper bells and balls were first used in 1908 to decorate the tree. They were also made in very large sizes in green or green and red combinations for use in hallways, on chandeliers, and/or on door frames. They usually were fitted with cardboard surrounds and could be folded flat for ease of storage. Some, made in the 1940s with multicolored cardboard stands, were used as table decorations, centerpieces or as fold-outs for greeting cards.

During the early part of the twentieth century, painted paper fans and umbrellas made in Japan were used as tree decorations. When they were not being used for ornaments, these pieces of paper became play toys and dolls. Also, since the early part of the twentieth century multicolored wax candles in figural form have been manufactured. Made as angels, Santas, reindeer, choir boys and girls or Christmas trees, they can be found at tag sales, often in original boxes at nominal prices.

In the late nineteenth century, following Clement Moore's instructions, children used their own everyday wool or lisle stockings at the fireplace mantel for Santa Claus to fill with fruits and nuts or other small goodies. In the early twentieth century, printed cotton stockings with depictions of winter or Christmas scenes became commercially available. By the middle of the century, these were followed by prefilled net stockings having lithographed paper Santa Claus closures. Available today, they are even made for cats and dogs and might be a future collectible, if left intact.

Made in the late nineteenth century in the United States and in Ger-

Group of Christmas stockings.
COURTESY OF SKINNER AUCTIONS.

many for export, cornucopias, in ice cream cone or stylized triangular shapes, were the first styles of candy container made to decorate the tree. They were constructed of paper or cardboard with scrap or die cut decoration, usually depicting Santa or angels' heads and enhanced with tinsel or glitter. Common for decorating trees, most were commercially made, although some were homemade. Many were gifts to children from their Sunday school teachers. In 1912, simple cornucopias decorated with paper poinsettas and holly leaves became popular.

At this same time period, larger papier-mâché, cardboard, and/or composition figural candy containers were commercially produced in Germany. They were first used as candy containers on trees, then later for table, mantel or window decorations. Sometimes they found service as toys, especially during or after the holiday. A variety of forms were popular including the Belsnickle, Father Christmas, farm animals or snow men, fish, all types of fruit made from wax-coated papier-mâché to resemble real fruit, oysters, chickens, turkeys, ducks, roosters with dyed feathers, wings, tails and wire legs, rabbits, dogs, pigs, and cats. Reindeer with cloth bodies, the best examples having horn antlers and leather bridles, were also manufactured. Some of the better styles of animals had blown glass eyes. Elves with woolen beards, full-figure Santas in chenille boots or individual full-figure Santas on yule logs formed the basis for a number of other candy containers. Often the head was able to be

Left, *Father Christmas candy container and nodder, circa 1900, papier-mâché face and hands, $2,200; right, early 20th-century Santa figure holding feather tree and wreath with bells.* COURTESY OF TERRY AND JOE DZIADUL.

removed for placing candy in the cardboard receptacle. Some had removable bases or other body parts. Others separated at the bottom of the coat, the top of the boots or at the waist. Most of the Santa or Kris Kringle figures wore red clothing and carried a tree. An unusual candy container was the champagne bottle, complete with paper label, used for both Christmas and New Year's. A rare cardboard candy container is in the form of a flower pot with holly decoration containing a small feather tree. Papier-mâché or mica-covered cardboard snow men were also made as individual figures for table, mantel or window decorations, complete just as the candy containers would be with top hats, canes, carrot noses, and sometimes holding a broom, feather tree or branch.

In the early twentieth century, a variety of paper and cardboard candy containers in various forms became popular. Sometimes referred to as candy boxes, these printed receptacles were also in a variety of forms including musical instruments; cat and dog figures; Santa Claus on top of a box in the shape of a house, sometimes with red cellophane windows; Santa on a chimney or in an airplane; various styles of houses or churches; a mantelpiece with lithographed stockings and a faux working fireplace; automobiles with cardboard wheels; sleighs; and sleighs pulled by reindeer. Folding candy boxes in square shapes had lithographed patterns depicting holly, Santa Claus, Christmas trees or chimneys with Santa. These were made in Germany, Japan, and the United States and often had doubled handles. By the 1930s and '40s, cardboard and papier-mâché containers mirrored popular Disney characters of the day. Mica-covered Snow White and the Seven Dwarfs was one group of many that were created.

Pressed or molded figural clear glass candy containers were produced in the latter part of the nineteenth and early part of the twentieth centuries, most often in America. In the form of animals, Santas, cartoon characters or houses, they were usually commercially filled with candy and able to be purchased at the dime or variety store.

During the 1920s, lithographed tins with Christmas motifs were made in England and the United States. Some of the most desirable were made by Huntley and Palmer. Manufactured in a variety of sizes and shapes including round, rectangular, and octagonal form, tins were made to hold cakes, cookies or chocolates. The tins depict a variety of scenes such as winter, Santa, carolers or skiers. Christmas tins with handles that could be used as lunch boxes after the holiday were also made.

At the turn of the twentieth century, Mayo's Tobacco issued lithographed tins in the form of a roly-poly Santa Claus with tobacco inside. After the tobacco was smoked, the children of the family played with these figures. Today roly-poly Santas, especially those in mint condition, are eagerly sought by collectors.

Carved wooden cookie molds were made in Germany during the early

Group of Schoenhut Santa roly-polys. COURTESY OF MARY AND BOB SCHNEIDER.

and middle part of the nineteenth century. Today they are being widely and wildly reproduced. Other types of molds became popular at the turn of the twentieth century. These included full-figure tin and pewter molds made for chocolate or ice cream, most made in Germany. In the early twentieth century, the Griswold Manufacturing Co. was producing cast-iron molds in similar figural shapes in America. Both in Germany and the United States, the figures most commonly produced were Santas, reindeers, Christmas trees, and angels. By the middle part of the twentieth century, aluminum cake and Jell-O molds in the shape of Christmas trees, Santas, and reindeer were being manufactured in large quantities.

In the early part of the twentieth century, brightly colored cast-iron figural doorstops depicting Santa Claus were produced. One example has Santa holding a tree; in another he is pictured with a sack of toys. Also, cast-iron banks with brightly decorated full-figure Santas or Santa sitting in a chair were just two of many examples that were produced at this same time period.

Lithographed prints manufactured in Germany and America, some by Maud Humphrey, in the late nineteenth and early twentieth centuries, were made for books, newspapers, calendars or magazine covers. Others were made as pictures to be framed. They often depicted such scenes as families at Christmas dinner, children with animals or Christmas stockings or Santa in various poses. Printed handkerchiefs and scarves manufactured at the same time are rare today and must be in perfect condition to retain their value.

Other printed material with Christmas motifs made from the latter part of the nineteenth century to the present day includes children's books, almost always with colored covers and colored lithographs. Two of the most prolific publishers were Tuck and McLaughlin. *Jolly Santa Claus,*

A Gift From Saint Nicholas, and *The Robin's Christmas Eve* are some of the popular books but, by far, the most popular of all time is *The Night Before Christmas*. Through the years, numbers of pages have been cut from individual books making them suitable for framing. Only those books with multiple colorful illustrations and all their pages intact are valuable. Other types of books were available in the 1920s and '30s and have become collectible today. Dennison offered a Christmas book similar to their books for the other holiday celebrations that offered suggestions for decorating and holiday preparations. In the 1940s, the Whitman Publishing Co. sold holiday books, the most popular being those with pop-up Santa Claus figures. Lithographed blocks and puzzles were also made at this same time period and depicted Santa, his elves, children, and Christmas scenes. The blocks were often enclosed in their own wooden or pressed cardboard boxes and had different scenes on each of their four sides. Both the blocks and the puzzles, in addition to being in their original boxes, should be in as close to mint condition as possible in order to rise in, and retain, value.

Lithographed Christmas postcards were made in the late nineteenth century in the United States, Germany, and England. Popular artists who designed the cards for manufacturers, such as Tuck and McLaughlin, were Frances Brundage, Ellen Clapsaddle, Rose O'Neill, and Palmer Cox. The most popular cards portrayed children hanging stockings and holding baby animals; Father Christmas; Santa Claus; holly and bells; Santa

Group of late 19th- and early 20th-century Christmas cards.
COURTESY OF SKINNER AUCTIONS.

in hot air balloons, sleighs or automobiles; elves; winter scenes; Christmas trees; angels; wreaths; snow babies; Kewpies; Brownies; and Kate Greenaway figures. Some were sold in series and hold-to-light examples were also made. Huge quantities of cards were manufactured and many have survived. Some collectors limit their search to particular styles of cards, such as Santa in cars or just Santas. Others look for cards by particular artists or those with hold-to-light features.

When postage became less expensive in the 1930s and '40s, printed greeting cards with their own envelopes became popular. For the most part, these greeting cards do not yet seem to have become universally popular. The only area that seems to garner a great deal of interest today is the card with Cubist-type Art Deco stylization.

At the turn of the twentieth century, colored lithographed trade cards, about the same size or a little larger than postcards, were given away by merchants as good-will gestures to remind people to buy their products throughout the year. These generally depicted winter, Santa or Christmas scenes on one side with the advertising imprint on the reverse.

Using the Santa Claus figure as an advertising spokesperson began in the latter part of the nineteenth century and continued through the 1960s. Beginning with the Mayo Tobacco roly-poly tin and ads for Pear's Soap, Santa has been a popular figure to help sell various products. Pages from early twentieth-century magazines with Santa Claus offering a bottle of Coke, cardboard stand-up Santa Claus figures advertising Coca-Cola and other products and used as counter or store displays are all collectible. Other products to use Santa included Whitman's candy, General Electric, and Noma lights. Some banks gave away calendars with Santas on them or small lithographed Santas suitable for hanging on the tree complete with hanger and the bank's logo on the back. Mechanical Santa figures were used in store advertising; and even greeting card companies, such as Gibson, used Santa to sell Christmas cards.

The Dennison paper company manufactured large quantities of party decorating supplies in the early part of the twentieth century. Some of the products, most often in red and green, included honeycomb bells, printed tablecloths with matching napkins, paper plates, and cups, invitations, place cards, nut cups with holly or mistletoe decoration, and crepe paper streamers. Full-figure cardboard depictions of Santa Claus in a sled, and even snow men, were made as centerpieces. Party favors included English paper crackers (snappers) which, when pulled, revealed paper hats and whistles. For wall decorations, pressed cardboard, color lithographed figures depicting Santa with a sack of toys, on the rooftop or the chimney, or just the head of Santa were also manufactured. One party-goer might have dressed as Santa. The costume including the mask, made from paper, rubber or composition, is collectible today.

Sheet music in mint condition from the 1930s, with colored litho-

Early 20th-century Santa party game. COURTESY OF MARY AND BOB SCHNEIDER.

Two Santa wall hangings, handpainted on velvet, 1930s, made for Macy's store display; left, *$350,* right, *$500.* COURTESY OF SKINNER AUCTIONS.

graphed scenes on the cover, are becoming collectible today. The most popular depict Bing Crosby singing "Silent Night" or "White Christmas." Early copies of "Rudolph the Red-Nosed Reindeer" sheet music are also collectible.

Christmas seals began to be used in the United States in 1907. They were first produced for the American Red Cross and then for tuberculosis associations. Printed in color, these decorative stamps depict Christmas scenes, some with Santa.

From the late nineteenth century until the 1930s in the United States, Gorham and Webster manufactured sterling silver spoons with depictions of Santa on the handles. These included Santa in a Christmas tree with a pack of toys or in a chimney. Others depicted holly and mistletoe with enamel decoration, the night before Christmas or one with a stocking at the top. Michelson Silver Co. of Denmark introduced a series of Christmas spoons in the early part of the twentieth century. Each year the company produced the spoons with a different scene on the handle, such as the Star of Bethlehem, bells, The Little Match Girl or a gift-laden Christmas tree, usually with enamel embellishment.

Most sterling silver tree ornaments are contemporary. Produced by Gorham, Reed and Barton, and Hallmark in America, the ornaments, usually flat, depict angels, bells, snowflakes, and animals and include the name of the ornament with its date engraved on one side. They were also made in Portugal, most often in full-figure form, for export to the United States.

Usually purchased as souvenirs, snow domes or shakers are one of the most recent collectibles. First made in the 1920s, they were clear glass balls enclosing figures such as Santas, Santas with reindeer and sleds, reindeer alone, Christmas carolers or snow men. The crystal ball was secured to a base and, when the piece was turned upside down, "snow" fell. Domes continue to be made today, most often with plastic covers. Through the years children have loved to watch the snow fall when the dome, its figure, and base were shaken.

In the early part of the twentieth century, various pieces of jewelry—particularly pins, usually with enamel decoration over sterling silver—were manufactured in rectangular shape with holly or mistletoe motifs. In the 1930s, pins with Santa heads, branches of holly or bells were produced in Bakelite. After World War II, brightly colored plastic pins were manufactured with Christmas bells that moved, holly with movable berries, Christmas trees with ornaments, and Santa Claus heads with jingle bells attached.

For more information regarding Christmas ornament collectibles, a new organization for collectors is the New England Ornament Collectors Club. They can be reached at: Three Cheers Hallmark, 1231 East Main Street, Meriden, CT 06450.

Christmas Listings

Advertising, book matches, Santa and elves, mid-20th century, Coca-Cola. $10

Advertising, paper wreath, die cut, "Drink Coca-Cola," early 20th century. $750

Advertising, poster paper, Santa Claus in front of fireplace advertising Coca-Cola, mid-20th century. $15

Advertising, Santa Claus Coca-Cola doll, rubber, red felt suit, holding a bottle of Coke, 17 inches high. $35

Advertising, Santa cloth-dressed figure, life-size, electric, from Reed's Drug Store. $950

Advertising, Santa on roof with toys, mechanical, department store, papier-mâché. $150

Advertising, Santa store window display, Santa's head atop chimney, paper and wood, clockwork mechanism, 20 inches tall. $350

Angel, Dresden, spun glass wings, wax, 4 inches. $250

Angel, tree top, cardboard with spun glass body, 1940s. $45

Angel, wax, circa 1900, missing hands, 4-inch diameter. $75

Angel, wax, circa 1900, new clothes, hands have been repaired, 5½-inch diameter. $150

Angels, two, German, early 20th century, wax over composition, gilded wings, fine condition, slight cracking, missing musical instruments. $175/2

Angel top, with spun glass hair and skirt, 1940. .... $45

Animal, deer, painted lead, circa 1930. .... $35

Animal, goat, rubber, 1940. .... $10

Animal, plastic, horse, Japanese, mid-20th century. $7

Animal, sheep, rubber, 1930. .... $10

Animals, blown glass, three, circa 1920; stork, 6 inches high, near mint; deer, 5 inches high, with clear base, small chip off mouth, base has one crack; pheasant, 3¼ inches high, near mint; deer and pheasant, multicolored, Germany. $225/3

Animals, sheep, bisque, early 20th century. $75

Animals, 20, celluloid, circa 1940, five marked "Occupied Japan," near mint. $225/lot

Bank, Santa Claus, asleep in chair, pot metal, early 20th century. $35

Bank, Santa Claus, battery operated, mid-20th century, lithographed tin. $150

Bank, Santa Claus, chalkware, early 20th century. $95

Bank, Santa Claus, holding tree, cast iron, early 20th century, 5½ inches high. $350

Bank, Santa Claus, in chair, chalkware, early 20th century. $50

Bank, Santa Claus, mid-20th century, painted plaster, 12 inches high. $35

Bank, Santa Claus, on top of chimney, red, chalkware, 10½ inches high. . $75

Bank, Santa Claus, papier-mâché, early 20th century, painted, 7½ inches high. $25

Bank, Santa holding Christmas tree, cast-iron reproduction. $10

Bank, Santa in chair, mid-20th century, plaster, 7 inches high. $25

Bank, Santa with Christmas tree, cast-iron reproduction. $10

Banner, cotton, stenciled "Merry Christmas," early 20th century, good condition. $125

Basket, printed cardboard with sewn panels, mid-20th century. $15

Basket, Santa and helpers, lithographed cardboard, German, 1930. .... $22

Group of early 20th-century Christmas collectibles including embossed album, advertising Santa, and tree stands. COURTESY OF GARTH'S AUCTIONS.

Mid-20th-century Santa advertising pieces. COURTESY OF JOAN AND ALLAN LEHNER.

Early 20th-century advertising Santa.
COURTESY OF JOAN AND ALLAN LEHNER.

Group of Belsnickle and Father Christmas figures. COURTESY OF JOAN AND
ALLAN LEHNER.

Bell, cardboard, foil covered, mid-20th century, Japanese. $5
Bell, foil-covered cardboard, Japanese, mid-20th century. $10
Bell, paper, red and green honeycomb tissue, 14-inch diameter. $15
Bells, white cardboard, 1940. .... $10
Belsnickle, early 20th century, molded and painted figure wearing white outfit sprinkled with mica, black boots, nose rubbed, height 8⅛ inches. $575
Belsnickle, early 20th century, molded painted papier-mâché figure wearing white cloak with mica flakes, black boots and base, carrying feather tree, minor wear, height 6½ inches. $525
Belsnickle, early 20th century, papier-mâché molded and painted figure wearing white cloak, decorated with mica flakes, black boots and base, carrying feather tree, fine facial features, fine condition, minor rubbing, height 7½ inches.
....$425
Belsnickle, early 20th century, papier-mâché, molded and painted figure, yellow coat and black boots, on wooden base, good condition, tree missing, height 10¼ inches. $975
Belsnickle, Father Christmas, German, gold with glitter, black base with snow, holding feather tree, pipe cleaner trim, 14 inches. $900
Belsnickle, Father Christmas, painted papier-mâché and gesso, glitter, paper bottom, holding feather tree, white with gold trim, fur hat trim, 13 inches.
.... $1,200
Bird, celluloid, early 20th century. $50
Book, *A Visit From Santa Claus*, McLaughlin, early 20th century. $60
Book, *Christmas Box, The*. $22
Book, coloring, *Santa Claus*, 1950. .... $10
Book, Dennison's *Christmas Book*, 1930. .... $18
Book, *Night Before Christmas*, early 20th century. $35
Book, Santa Claus, *Fuzzy Wuzzy*, mid-20th century. $35

Book, scrap, embossed cover with four Santas in color, marked "patent March 1876," filled with colorful lithographed printed cut-outs, embossed seals, advertising cards, and postcards. $125

Booklet, seals, Currier and Ives decoration. $5

Bookmark, felt, embroidered "Merry Christmas," handmade, late 19th century. $35

Bookmark, leather, Christmas tree and "Season's Greetings," circa 1900. .... $10

Boot, foil-covered paper with Santa on top, Japanese, 1930. ....$35

Cake tin, Santa Claus, tin, early 20th century, 9 inches high. $85

Calendar, lithographed paper, family around Christmas tree, dated 1912. . $35

Candle, wax, Santa Claus, 12 inches high, mid-20th century. $22

Candle, wax, choir boy, mid-20th century. $3

Candle clips, tin, 17, decorated, early 20th century. $75/all

Candle holder, bird with balance, early 20th century. $175

Candle holder, clip-on butterfly, early 20th century. $125

Candle holder, clip-on counterbalance. $25

Candle holder, clip-on flower form, early 20th century. $75

Candle holder, clip-on fruit, tin, early 20th century. $90

Candle holder, clip-on glass figural rose, early 20th century. $150

Candle holder, clip-on glass flower form, early 20th century. $125

Candle holder, fairy lamp, amber pressed glass, early 20th century. $35

Candle holder, four-sided hanging, early 20th century. $75

Candle holder, glass pine cone with balance, early 20th century. $175

Candle holder, lantern, Father Christmas, papier-mâché, full-figure head with wire bale handle, early 20th century. $450

Candle holder, lantern, hanging isinglass, late 19th century. $110

Candle holder, wooden Christmas tree shaped with cross base, wire arms, original paint, repairs, 24 inches high. $95

Candle holders, clip-on, tin with crimped cups, set of 12. ....$55/set

Candle holders, group, late 19th–early 20th century, tin, 13 counterbalance holders, 23 clip-on. $100/all

Candle shades, lot of four, lithographed paper shades revolve from heat, early 20th century. $75/4

Candlesticks, pair of holly branches, cast iron, painted holders, mid-20th century, Japanese. $25/pr

Candy box, blue and green cardboard, die cut scrap decoration, early 20th century. $35

Candy box, butterfly, cardboard, green and white, early 20th century. $25

Group of late 19th-century glass and tin candle holders for tree.
COURTESY OF MARGARET SCOTT CARTER.

Mid-20th-century cardboard candy boxes. COURTESY OF JOAN AND ALLAN LEHNER.

Candy box, Dresden cardboard football, early 20th century. $175
Candy box, Dresden cardboard football, small. $110
Candy box, Dresden guitar, pink and purple applied decoration. $200
Candy box, Dresden guitar, tan, early 20th century. $175
Candy box, Dresden guitar, white, large. $175
Candy box, Dresden, with dove and heart, early 20th century. $325
Candy box, green and white lithographed cardboard, mid-20th century. ... $15
Candy box, purple cardboard, gold embossed paper lace frill, early 20th century. $35
Candy box, Santa Claus on zeppelin holding stars and stripes, cardboard. $225
Candy box, Santa in chenille boot, Japan, early 20th century, 8½ inches high. $100
Candy box, Santa in chimney, Fanny Farmer, 1930s, lithographed cardboard. $35
Candy box, Santa in sleigh, lithographed cardboard, Germany, 1930. .....$135
Candy box, Santa in sleigh, lithographed cardboard, Japanese, 1930, large size. $125
Candy box, Santa, painted papier-mâché, early 20th century, 9 inches high. $275
Candy box, Santa, sitting beside Christmas tree, circa 1930, molded cardboard. $275
Candy box, tambourine shape, cardboard, circa 1940. .... $35
Candy box, village building, American, 1940, lithographed cardboard. $35
Candy container, angel holding feather tree, papier-mâché, early 20th century, German. $225
Candy container, banjo, red paper, early 20th century, German. $75
Candy container, bell, white papier-mâché, early 20th century, Germany, 5-inch diameter. $75
Candy container, Belsnickle, blue, circa 1890, new base, feet missing, 6 inches high. $125
Candy container, Belsnickle, circa 1890, red, bottom missing, 6½ inches high. $175

Early 20th-century molded cardboard candy containers. COURTESY OF JOAN AND ALLAN LEHNER.

Candy container, Belsnickle, late 19th century, white robe, covered with glitter, mint condition, 7¾ inches high. $525
Candy container, Belsnickle, late 19th century, dressed in white with black boots, Christmas tree missing, 10 inches high. $475
Candy container, Belsnickle, late 19th century, Germany, figure in mica-covered white coat, band of red fabric, black boots, in good original condition, no longer opens, height 20¾ inches. $3,750
Candy container, Belsnickle, red coat holding feather tree, papier-mâché, early 20th century, German, 8 inches. $650
Candy container, Belsnickle, red, marked "Germany," late 19th century, mint condition, 5¾ inches high. $425
Candy container, Belsnickle, white coat, papier-mâché, early 20th century, German, 11 inches high. $950
Candy container, boot, papier-mâché and glitter, mid-20th century. $50
Candy container, boot, papier-mâché, red with holly trim, early 20th century. $50
Candy container, boots, red composition, 1940s. $15
Candy container, boots, red composition, 1940s, good condition. $25
Candy container, chenille bell with cotton batting, 1920. ....$125
Candy container, church with removable steeple, lithographed cardboard, early 20th century. $75
Candy container, cornucopia, blue paper, late 19th century, German. $25
Candy container, Dresden cardboard chair, embossed gold paper lace trim. $150
Candy container, Dresden parrot head with feather decoration, cardboard. $375
Candy container, Dresden pipe, cardboard with tinsel wrapping. $150
Candy container, Dresden football, seamed with stitches. $75
Candy container, Dresden sleigh, cardboard, embossed lace and chenille roping. $225

Candy container, drum with die cut lithograph decoration, early 20th century. $75

Candy container, Father Christmas, blue robe, papier-mâché, feet repaired, German, early 20th century. $350

Candy container, Father Christmas, German, painted papier-mâché, gesso face, hands and feet, wood base, holding feather tree, cloth robe, glitter rabbit fur, 27 inches high. $1,750

Candy container, Father Christmas, Germany, early 20th century, mica covered, 10 inches. $900

Candy container, Father Christmas, red and green papier-mâché, early 20th century, feet repaired. $110

Candy container, fireplace with hanging stockings, lithographed cardboard, Japanese, 1930. .... $75

Candy container, Krampus, paper, Germany, early 20th century. $375

Candy container, parasol, wooden handle, embossed lace trim. $150

Candy container, Pere Noel, papier-mâché, Continental, 24 inches. ... $1,000

Candy container, Pere Noel, white and gold, early 20th century, Continental, 10 inches. $750

Candy container, piano, Steinway, lithographed cardboard, early 20th century. $250

Candy container, reindeer, papier-mâché, blown glass eyes, neck closure, 6 inches high. $350

Candy container, reindeer, removable head, German, early 20th century. $350

Candy container, Santa Claus in automobile, green moss over cardboard wheels, early 20th century, German, 5½-inch length. $950

Candy container, Santa Claus in chimney, cotton batting over cardboard, early 20th century. $125

Candy container, Santa Claus in sleigh with tree and yule logs, papier-mâché and cardboard, bog moss decoration, early 20th century, German. $950

Candy container, Santa Claus in sleigh, bisque face, early 20th century, Japanese. $550

Candy container, Santa Claus on chimney, cotton batting body, mid-20th century. $65

Left, *pair of early 20th-century reindeer candy containers;* right, *Santa on chimney top candy container.* COURTESY OF JOAN AND ALLAN LEHNER.

Early 20th-century candy container with bisque hands and net-covered body, $70.
COURTESY OF BARB AND DICK SHILVOCK.

Candy container, Santa Claus on chimney, lithographed cardboard, mid-20th century. $35

Candy container, Santa Claus on rooftop, lithographed cardboard, mid-20th century, 9 inches high. $75

Candy container, Santa Claus on sleigh with reindeer, head of reindeer removable, papier-mâché and cardboard, late 19th century, German. $850

Candy container, Santa Claus on sleigh, papier-mâché, late 19th century, German, small size. $175

Candy container, Santa Claus, papier-mâché, red paint, marked patent applied for, early 20th century, 9 inches high. $125

Candy container, Santa Claus standing by chimney, lithographed cardboard. $75

Candy container, Santa Claus and sleigh with reindeer, Germany, 10-inch length. $1,390

Candy container, Santa Claus, bisque head, holding sack of toys, early 20th century, 8 inches. $600

Candy container, Santa Claus, body opens in center, papier-mâché, early 20th century. $110

Candy container, Santa Claus, clear glass, painted plastic head, mid-20th century, 6 inches. $35

Candy container, Santa Claus, climbing into chimney, glass, circa 1920, 5 inches. $125

Candy container, Santa Claus, felt clothes, bisque face, Japanese, early 20th century, 5 inches. $150

Candy container, Santa Claus, German, early 20th century, molded composition, painted face, together with German composition Santa Claus on wooden seat, 12 inches high. $800/2

Candy container, Santa Claus, holding feather tree in hand, papier-mâché, Germany, 11 inches. $950

Candy container, Santa Claus, in boot, mesh bag over shoulder, Japan, 6 inches high. $100

Candy container, Santa Claus, nodder, lithographed paper, mid-20th century. $75

Candy container, Santa Claus, on wooden log sleigh, feather tree, Germany, early 20th century, 5 inches. $550

Candy container, Santa Claus, original red paint, worn condition, mid-20th century, Japanese. $20

Candy container, Santa Claus, plastic head, glass body. $35

Candy container, Santa Claus, pressed cardboard face, chenille-covered wire body, mid-20th century. $45

Candy container, Santa Claus, red felt coat, rabbit fur beard, 1950s, 10 inches high. $95

Candy container, Santa Claus, white suit, red trim, molded cardboard, early 20th century. $75

Candy container, Santa driving an auto, early 20th century, Germany, bisque head, blown glass eyes, closed mouth, papier-mâché and red cloth body, white cardboard open car, mica finish and holly trim, back of car opens to hold candy, 7½ inches × 7⅜ inches. ....:...................$750

Candy container, Santa holding feather tree, fur beard, mid-20th century. $75

Candy container, Santa in chimney, head first, lithographed cardboard, early 20th century. $75

Candy container, Santa on log, paper and composition, 1920, Germany. ..../...........$275

Candy container, Santa on motorcycle, celluloid, early 20th century, Japanese, 5-inch length. $250

Candy container, Santa on sleigh with two papier-mâché reindeer, German, early 20th century, 12-inch length. $650

Candy container, Santa's boot, plastic, mid-20th century, Japanese. $10

Candy container, Santa, circa 1900, celluloid face, composition hands, brown robe, black boots, mint condition, 6½ inches high. $300

Candy container, Santa, composition, on sled, German, early 20th century. $125

Candy container, Santa, early 20th century, Germany, molded papier-mâché face and hands, rabbit fur beard, red flannel robe, good condition, replaced legs and base, tree missing, height 10¾ inches. $250

Candy container, Santa, German, early 20th century, molded head, cloth and papier-mâché body, sitting on cylindrical container, back of right arm stained, height 8 inches. $400

Candy container, Santa, late 19th century, Germany, papier-mâché and cloth, standing figure, original condition, height 6½ inches. $175

Candy container, slipper, cardboard, red velvet covered with beaded trim, late 19th century, German. $150

Candy container, snow baby on sled, cardboard base. $175

Candy container, snow man, papier-mâché, marked "Germany," early 20th century. $125

Candy container, snow man, papier-mâché, top hat, holding branch, German, early 20th century. $110

Candy container, snow man, papier-mâché, white, red, and black, worn, 6¾ inches high. $25

Candy container, tambourine, cardboard, early 20th century, small size. . $75

Candy container, walnut, embossed and colored cardboard. $65

Candy container, Santa, 20th century, Germany and Japan, including figures of cloth and cardboard with papier-mâché faces, three standing, two sitting, height 3⅞ to 5 inches; Santa standing on crenelated roof of small castle, top lifts off to hold candy, height 7½ inches. $200/all

Left, *early 20th-century snow man candy container with bottle-brush tree.* COURTESY OF JOAN AND ALLAN LEHNER. Right, *group of mid-20th-century Disney candy containers.* PRIVATE COLLECTION.

Group of early 20th-century candy containers. COURTESY OF SKINNER AUCTIONS.

Group of early 20th-century candy containers. COURTESY OF SKINNER AUCTIONS.

Candy containers, Santa, two, Japan, 1930s, celluloid faces, cloth hats and arms, papier-mâché hands and feet, with net bag top, height 6 inches, net bag forms body of second Santa, height 8¾ inches. $130/2

Candy containers, Santas, two, early 20th-century standing figures, papier-mâché heads, hands, and feet, cloth robes, rabbit fur beards (trees missing), 7¾ inches. $475/2

Candy containers, two, Victorian girl dressed in red hat and coat with white trim and Belsnickle dressed in pink (damage), early 20th century. $250/2

Card, children with decorated tree, late 19th century. $10

Card, Christmas, homemade, cloth, paper, watercolor, red tassel, large. .. $25

Card, floral Christmas scene, lithographed, Prang. $20

Card, floral silk fringe, Prang, lithographed, late 19th century. $15

Card, Mouseketeer Christmas cards, mint in box, 1950s. $30

Card, movable, late 19th century, bird and birdhouse, lithographed paper. $25

Card, village scene, opens to honeycomb tissue insert, early 20th century, faded condition. $15

Carpet, tree, lithographed canvas depicting Santa in sleigh with reindeer and trees. $135

Carpet, tree, painted fabric depicting Santa and village. $150

Centerpiece, Santa in carriage with parasol, straw, lace, and tin, early 20th century, German, 9-inch length. $1,200

Centerpiece, Santa in reindeer-drawn sleigh, toys in sleigh, glass eyes, felt robe, leather bridle, bentwood frame, reindeer is candy container. $750

Centerpiece, Santa with reindeer and sleigh, painted papier-mâché on wood, early 20th century, German, 16-inch length. $850

Centerpiece, table, full-figure honeycomb tissue Santa Claus on cardboard base. $28

Centerpiece, table, honeycomb tissue Christmas bells on cardboard base, 1930s. $35

Cookie cutter, Christmas tree shape, tin, early 20th century. $15

Cookie cutter, Father Christmas, 19th century, tin, rare. $600

Cookie jar, Santa Claus head, pottery, 1940. .... $65

Cookie jar, Santa on rooftop, ceramic, mid-20th century. $25

Cornucopia, foil over cardboard, American, 1940. .... $25

Cornucopia, netting with die cut lithograph, early 20th century. $75

Early 20th-century honeycomb tissue paper and cardboard tree centerpieces. COURTESY OF JOAN AND ALLAN LEHNER.

Group of late 19th-century cardboard cornucopias hung on feather tree.

COURTESY OF JOAN AND ALLAN LEHNER.

Cornucopia, paper covered with netting and die cuts, early 20th century. . $75
Cornucopia, paper with gilt paper trim, early 20th century. $75
Cornucopia, tapered cardboard, four-sided, late 19th century, die cut trim.
.... $75
Costume, Santa Claus, with mask and beard, original box, mid-20th century.
.... $75
Cut-out, group of embossed paper with polychrome color and some glitter including four Santas, Santa and sleigh, Mary and Child in star, some with damage and wear. $75/all
Cut-out, stand-up Santa, embossed paper, mid-20th century, 11 inches high.
.... $15
Cut-out, stand-up Santa in sleigh, lithographed double-sided cardboard, mid-20th century, 8-inch length. $10
Cut-out, stand-up Santa, embossed and flocked paper, Germany, early 20th century, 11 inches high. $35
Decoration, bottle-brush tree, Japanese, 1930. ....$5
Decoration, box of artificial snow flakes, 1930s, poor condition. $10
Decoration, box of tinsel icicles, mid-20th century. $5
Decoration, camel, celluloid, large size. $35
Decoration, chain, interlocking paper, homemade, multicolor. $10
Decoration, deer, cast iron, five, circa 1910, height of the largest is 5 inches, three are standing, two are lying down, all are marked "Germany," minor flaking, nice condition. $100/5
Decoration, deer, cast iron, five, circa 1920, all excellent, minor flaking.
....$75/5
Decoration, donkey, nodder, celluloid, circa 1930, string needs replacing, 5½ inches high. $25
Decoration, pine cone, foil covered, 1940. ....$7

Early 20th-century Santa in rattan auto with Christmas trees. COURTESY OF JOAN AND ALLAN LEHNER.

Decoration, pine cone, foil covered, mid-20th century. $5
Decoration, reindeer, blown silvered glass, mid-20th century. $35
Decoration, Santa in car, celluloid, 1930. .... $75
Decoration, Santa, celluloid, early 20th century. $50
Decoration, tinsel rope garland, early 20th century, fair condition. $10
Decorations, including glass balls, boxes, figures, Santas, some lot damage. $250/all

Decorations, late 19th and early 20th centuries, three small Kugels, one red; blown glass: blue and white peacock, horns, nuts, fruit, indents, bead chain; metal stars, mirrors; 11 weighted and 25 tin clip-on candle holders, many with paint (damage and paint loss to lot). $150/all

Group of late 19th- and early 20th-century Christmas decorations including candy containers, embossed grape Kugels, molds, and prints.
COURTESY OF GARTH'S AUCTIONS.

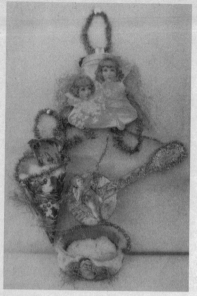

Group of die cut and tinsel-wrapped decorations. COURTESY OF BARB AND DICK SHILVOCK.

Die cut, angel, with feather wings and spun glass tail, early 20th century. . $50
Die cut, angel and Santa in circle, double face, early 20th century, German, tinsel surround. $35
Die cut, angel in circle, 1920, German. $10
Die cut, angel with wings and spun glass tail, early 20th century, German. $125
Die cut, butterfly with glitter trim, early 20th century, German. $50
Die cut, fan, early 20th century. $50
Die cut, fan in circle, early 20th century, German. $25
Die cut, moon face on clip, early 20th century, German, tinsel surround. . $50
Die cut, Santa double-faced in circle, early 20th century, German. $75
Die cut, Santa with paper costume and paper boots, 1920, German. $75
Die cuts, ten, mid-20th century, German, including embossed polychromed curch, snow man, house, three Santas, bell tower, lantern, candles, and pine cones, all with Merry Christmas greetings, pieces accented with mica snow and silver sparkles. $170/all
Die cuts, ten, mid-20th century, German, embossed, polychromed candles, house, bell, tower, two lanterns, snow man, church, three Santas, all with Merry Christmas greetings, pieces accented with mica snow and silver sparkles, eight measure 9¼ inches × 6½ inches; two are 13inches × 9¾ inches. $170/10
Doll, Santa, early 20th century, molded and painted face, straw-stuffed body and limbs, lambs wool beard, felt outfit (some fabric fading and wear), height 27 inches. $140
Doorstop, Santa, cast-iron reproduction. $45
Doorstop, Santa, cast iron, blown glass eyes, early 20th century. $150
Doorstop, Santa, cast iron, early 20th century, painted decoration, 8 inches high. $225
Doorstop, Santa, iron, early 20th century, 10½ inches high. $350
Doorstop, Santa, painted iron reproduction. $45

Doorstop, white metal, Santa Claus holding tree and toys, early 20th century. $225

Fence, brass Christmas tree, 14 sections, two gates, and 13 posts, worn pink paint, early 20th century. $200

Fence, cast-iron Gothic motif, late 19th century, German. $350

Fence, Christmas tree, wooden, seven sections, red and green turned gateposts, early 20th century. $85

Fence, goose feathers, five sections, made in Germany, 20th century. $375

Fence, red and green Strombeck-Berker, four sections in original box. ... $300

Fence, tin Christmas tree, green with red posts, five sections and a gate. . $175

Fence, twig with gates, early 20th century, German, small size. $75

Fence, wooden Christmas tree, faded green, white gate, one picket missing, early 20th century. $45

Fence, wooden Christmas tree, pickets with square posts, white paint with red trim, four sections and gate, some damage. $85

Fence, wooden, circa 1910, a couple of uprights missing and one post nail exposed, six pieces and two bridges, $3\frac{1}{4}$ inches $\times$ 9 inches. $75

Figure, Belsnickle, bisque, gray and black robe, pink face and white beard, chips and wear, $2\frac{1}{2}$ inches high. $35

Figure, Belsnickle, red paint with black and polychrome face, small feather tree in arm, some wear, minor paint flaking. $400

Figure, Belsnickle, white robe with glitter, 10 inches high, early 20th century, German. $600

Figure, camel, celluloid, 1930s. $35

Figure, Father Christmas holding toys, bisque head, early 20th century, $4\frac{1}{2}$ inches high. $175

Figure, Father Christmas, chalk blue paint with white trim, red trim around coat, holding switches, 15 inches high, early 20th century. $1,500

Figure, Father Christmas, painted papier-mâché, gesso face, hands and feet, felt and cotton clothes, reddish-brown coat and hat, rabbit fur trim, holding feather tree and net, 18 inches. $1,100

Figure, nodder, Father Christmas, wood base, painted papier-mâché, gesso face, hands and feet, felt clothes with rabbit fur trim, holding feather tree and basket, early 20th century, German, 29 inches high. $1,800

Figure, reindeer, silvered glass, 1940. .... $35

Figure, Santa Claus and sleigh, single reindeer, cotton batting figure, cardboard sleigh, early 20th century. $350

Figure, Santa Claus, celluloid face, mid-20th century, Japanese, 10 inches high. $145

Figure, Santa Claus, celluloid face, red flannel costume, green fiber tree, marked "made in Japan," mid-20th century, $6\frac{1}{2}$ inches high. $65

Figure, Santa Claus, painted chalk, early 20th century, German. $750

Figure, Santa Claus, papier-mâché, blue costume, early 20th century, 5 inches. $350

Figure, Santa in moss-covered cardboard sleigh, early 20th century. $750

Figure, Santa on bear, bisque, German. $125

Figure, Santa on sled, bisque, German, early 20th century. $75

Figure, Santa, chenille on cardboard base, Japanese, 1930s. $35

Figure, Santa, composition, seated in moss automobile, early 20th century. $850

Figure, Santa, cotton pipe cleaner, painted bisque face, fiber tree, faded color, mid-20th century, $5\frac{1}{4}$ inches high. $45

Left, *early 20th-century Christmas figure with feather tree on log sleigh with wooden runners;* right, *Father Christmas, circa 1900.* COURTESY OF JOAN AND ALLAN LEHNER.

Early 20th-century Father Christmas with feather tree and sleigh of packages. COURTESY OF JOAN AND ALLAN LEHNER.

Composition and paint Krampus figure. PRIVATE COLLECTION.

Figure, snow baby seated on ball, bisque, Japanese, circa 1930. .... $50
Figure, snow baby waving hands, bisque, Japanese, circa 1930. .... $45
Figure, snow baby, bisque, red coat, early 20th century. $85
Figures, creche, two, 19th-century Italian, man and boy, molded pottery heads with glass eyes, molded hands and feet, silk and cotton robes, fine condition, height 8 inches and 9¼ inches, wooden stands. $350/2
Figures, group, 20th century, including papier-mâché, plastic, plaster, cloth, some wind-up, some candy containers, celluloid Santa in sleigh pulled by two reindeer (some lot wear). $140/all
Figures, group, early 20th century, including four papier-mâché and cloth Santas, height 4½ inches; papier-mâché angel, length 3½ inches; two crepe paper and papier-mâché children, height 3¼ inches; two celluloid parrots (hoops missing, slight lot wear). $140/all
Figures, human, handpainted bisque, early 20th century, boxed. $150/set
Figures, Santa, four, 20th century, including two papier-mâché Belsnickles, height 3 inches, papier-mâché Santa, height 3 inches, all wooden bead animated Santa, height 7 inches. $75/4
Figures, Santas, six, mid-20th century, four of wire, cloth, and plastic, two have papier-mâché heads, two have plastic, synthetic fur-trimmed velvet outfits, lambs wool beards; one all papier-mâché, one all papier-mâché with molded head and jointed at the shoulders, flannel outfit together with Santa-form candle (some lot wear and damage). $120/all
Figures, Santas, two, flocked cardboard, plastic and fiber tree, pipe cleaner bodies, 6 inches high. $90/2
Figures, Santas, two, late 19th and early 20th centuries, cloth and wood figure turns somersaults over wooden posts, height 8⅜ inches, painted tin figure with hook on back, probably traveled on a string (paint fair), height 5¾ inches. $250/2
Flask, "A Merry Christmas/Happy New Year," woman sitting on a barrel, smoky aqua glass pint in the shape of a half-barrel, smooth base, tooled lip, unusual color, American, circa 1880–1900. .... $135
Flask, pocket, clear glass, colorful label under glass showing Santa Claus and wording "A Merry Christmas and a Happy New Year," ground lip, original cap, 6-inch height. $1,550

Left, *three early 20th-century pocket flasks;* right, *early 20th-century pocket flask depicting Santa, $1,600.* COURTESY OF GLASS WORKS AUCTION.

Flask, pocket, clear glass, colorful label under glass showing birds in a cherry tree and wording "A Merry Christmas/Happy New Year," ground lip, original cap, 4¾-inch height. $725

Flask, pocket, clear glass, colorful label under glass showing man with a bottle of 1891 rye and wording "A Merry Christmas/Corking Good Stuff/Happy New Year," ground lip, original cap, 6-inch height. $1,100

Flask, pocket, label under glass showing Santa Claus and wording "A Merry Christmas and Happy New Year," smooth base, ground lip, original cap, perfect, American, circa 1880–1910, 5⅞-inch height. $1,600

Game, Kris Kringle Bean Bag Board, lithographed cardboard, 17 inches high. $75

Game, The Visit of Santa Claus, McLaughlin, lithographed cardboard. $2,100

Garland, red tissue with tinsel trim, 35 feet. $15

Group, three pieces including two Santas, 2¾ inches and 3½ inches high, with pine cone bodies, crepe paper sack on cardboard stands marked "Germany East Zone," Santa with sleigh and two reindeer, all wood, marked "Germany," 4 inches × 3 inches, attractive, all very good condition. $120/all

Handkerchief, Santa Claus, printed cotton, Nast, mid-19th century. $550

Handkerchief, Santa, signed Oriental Print works, late 19th century, full-color Santa holding toys stands in the snow, vignettes of his visit depicted in the four corners of the cloth (some staining), 28½ inches × 17⅝ inches. $400

Handkerchief, St. Nicholas, printed cotton, faded condition. $345

Handkerchief, Thomas Nast lithographed picture, circa 1880. ....$375

Hooked rug, "Merry Christmas," dated 1929, very poor condition. $30

House, cardboard, foil covered, 1940. .... $10

Houses, cardboard with glitter trim, 1940. .... $15

Houses, cardboard, five, circa 1930, height of tallest is 5½ inches, marked "Japan," two have Santas on them, all are excellent to near mint. $125/all

A 19th-century printed cotton handkerchief, $400. COURTESY
OF SKINNER AUCTIONS.

Group of feather trees, fences, and embossed cardboard decorations.

COURTESY OF GARTH'S AUCTIONS.

Houses, cardboard, six, circa 1930, height of tallest is 5½ inches, these are larger and better detailed, each has a Santa or snow man in front, all mint to near mint, marked "Japan." $150/all

Houses, set, cardboard, painted glitter trim, circa 1940, Japanese. $125/set

Icicles, box, ribbon tinsel, mid-20th century, American. $15

Icicles, foil spiral with color, 1930, box. $25

Icicles, lead foil, early 20th century, box. $15

Icicles, plastic, mid-20th century, box. $5

Illustrations, three, framed, black and white, 19th century, "Santa Claus His Works" by Thomas Nast, 13½ inches × 20½ inches; "Christmas 1863" by Thomas Nast, 13½ inches × 20½ inches; "Nick Nax Pictorial 1858," 13⅝ inches × 20¾ inches (some paper discoloration on lot). $75/3

Jack-in-the-box, Santa Claus, celluloid face, cloth body, 1930, Japanese. $325

Jack-in-the-box, Santa Claus, early 20th century, Japanese. $125

Jug, Royal Doulton, Santa Claus, pottery, large size. $250

Kugel, embossed cap, gold, 5-inch diameter. $50

Kugel, green, brass cap, made in France, 7½-inch diameter. $475

Kugel, green, embossed cap, 4 inches. $60

Kugel, silver, embossed cap, 2½ inches. $25

Lamp, Christmas tree, glass, early 20th century, small size. $95

Lamp, Santa Claus, miniature, milk glass with painted red suit, facial features, boots and base, nutmeg burner, Consolidated Lamp & Glass Co., late 19th century, 9½ inches high. $4,500

Lamp, Santa fairy lamp, oil, handpainted milk glass, small chip on rim, 9½ inches high. $950

Lawn ornament, stick-up Santa and sleigh, printed paper on plywood, wear and damage, mid-20th century, 47 inches high. $50

Light bulb, bell, milk glass with Santa's face on it, circa 1930, red, green, blue, and black, slight flaking, 2½ inches high. $125

Light bulb, Santa, circa 1930s, red suit, orange bag, green pants, full figure, paint flaking, 3 inches high. $110

Light bulb, Santa, Japan, circa 1940, red, holding green tree, 5 inches high. $175

Light bulbs, comic characters, circa 1940, including Andy Gump, Betty Boop, Little Orphan Annie, and Smitty, multicolored, height 2½ inches. $425/all

Light bulbs, four, including parrot, and three lanterns with polychrome decoration, mid-20th century. $150/4

Light bulbs, lot of 44, 20th century, including Santa, snow men, birds, flowers, cottages, lanterns, paint loss to lot. $750/all

Light bulbs, rope of 12, porcelain sockets, early 20th century. $110

Lights, box set of Edison, early 20th century. $325

Lights, bubble, mid-20th century, boxed set. $75/set

Lights, fruit figurals, early, 1920s, box set. $300/set

Lights, German candles, early 1900s, box set. $425/set

Lights, Japanese-style houses, 1930s, box set. $75/set

Lights, Mickey Mouse, circa 1939, complete set, each has a plastic shade over it with decals of Disney characters, excellent condition. $550/set

Lights, Mickey Mouse, set and two chenille bells, Noma Electric Corp., 1950s, boxed string of eight bells decorated with decals of Mickey and other Disney characters, instructions; Japanese decorations with Santa heads on side, hanging fringe, height 3¼ inches. $250/all

Lights, milk glass figures, Japanese, 1930s, box set. $95/all

Early 20th-century Christmas lights in original boxes. COURTESY OF JOAN AND ALLAN LEHNER.

Group of early 20th-century Christmas collectibles. COURTESY OF SALLIE
AND BOB CONNELLY.

Lights, milk glass, three, circa 1930, one dirigible, one frog, one Santa head.
.... $250/3
Lights, Noma bubble, two sets, circa 1945, nine bubble lights on string, boxes
in very good condition, bulbs work. $18/2
Lights, Santa, two in original bases, marked "Japan," circa 1930, colorful, red
robe, handpainted toys, working, near mint, both lights show virtually no wear,
9½-inch base. $125/2
Lights, two, circa 1930, milk glass dirigibles in red, white, blue, yellow, and
green, light wear and flaking, 2¾ inches long. $200/2
Lights, Walt Disney character, circa 1960, two sets, one by Diamond Brite, one
by Paramount, both mint in the box, characters are handpainted milk glass.
....$35/2

Lithograph, Santa, framed, colored, late 19th century, Santa dressed all in white
holds toys in left hand, walking stick in right (paper damage), 11¹³/₁₆ inches ×
9⅝ inches. $100
Lot, circa 1920, including German village scene with church and seven other
buildings, church is 5⅜ inches high to steeple, 5⅛ inches wide, 2¼ inches deep,
most stamped "Germany," some buildings need attention, two metal reindeer
marked "Germany," bottle-brush tree, Santa marked "Germany," beard replaced. $100/lot
Lunch box, Santa Claus, nursery rhymes, lithographed tin, mid-20th century.
....$120
Mask, Santa Claus, painted paper, cotton beard, early 20th century. $125
Mask, Santa Claus, papier-mâché, polychrome with cotton batting beard, Ger-
many, early 20th century. $250
Mold, Belsnickle, cast aluminum, 8¼ inches high. $55
Mold, cake, Santa Claus, Griswold, iron, early 20th century. $375

Mold, chocolate, four Santas, full figure, tin, made in Germany. $225
Mold, chocolate, Santa Claus, early 20th century. $75
Mold, chocolate, Santa Claus, single, tin, early 20th century, German. $25
Mold, chocolate, Santa Claus, tin, late 19th century, German. $250
Mold, cookie, wooden, multiple Christmas trees, early 20th century, German.
....$125
Mold, ice cream, Santa Claus, full figure with pack of toys, pewter, early 20th century. $75
Mold, Rudolph the Red-Nosed Reindeer, cast aluminum, mid-20th century.
.... $12
Napkin ring, figural, reindeer pulling cart, silverplate, American, circa 1880.
....$350
Nativity, animals, plaster, group of five, Italian, 1930. ....$100/all
Nativity, sheep and goats, wool, plaster, and wood, early 20th century, group of six. $200/all
Nativity scene, cardboard, original box, mid-20th century. $50
Nativity scene, carved wood and pressed paper, late 19th century, German, original box. $125
Nativity scene, contemporary, plastic, West Germany. $10
Nativity scene, papier-mâché with animals, 15 pieces, German, early 20th century. $150
Nativity scene, papier-mâché, Germany, circa 1880, six figures and wax baby Jesus, some repairs and breaks. $75
Nativity scene, pressed cardboard, 1940s. $45
Novelty, foil-covered ornament, American, 1940. ....$5
Novelty, foil-covered pine cone, German, 1930. .... $10
Novelty, snowflakes, plastic, American, mid-20th century, boxed. $10
Nutcracker, Santa Claus head, wooden, painted red and gold, late 19th century.
....$250
Ornament, airplane with wheels, wire wrapped, glass. $325
Ornament, airplane with wire tinsel and bisque Santa with scrap face, unsilvered, 7¼ inches. $125
Ornament, airplane, bright pink wire-wrapped glass. $165
Ornament, airplane, glass, circa 1920, pink, near mint, very rare, 4½ inches wide. $375
Ornament, airplane, glass, circa 1920, white, near mint, very rare, 4½ inches wide. $325
Ornament, airship, glass with gold crochet, with boy. $175
Ornament, angel, crepe skirt. $150
Ornament, angel head on clip, glass. $75
Ornament, angel head with Dresden trim, flat. $225
Ornament, angel head with gold hair and red cheeks, glass. $125
Ornament, angel in moon, Dresden, flat. $275
Ornament, angel in tinsel sunburst, die cut scrap. $75
Ornament, angel on flying goose, bisque. $125
Ornament, angel with folded wings, kneeling, glass, circa 1900, red wings, silver body, minor tarnishing. $175
Ornament, angel with molded wings, pink-gold hair, glass. $125
Ornament, angel with paper skirt. $125
Ornament, angel with red wings, glass. $175
Ornament, angel with silver wings, Dresden, flat. $150
Ornament, angel, composition with Dresden trim. $225

Ornament, angel, composition, wax. $175
Ornament, angel, sterling silver, Portuguese, contemporary. $75
Ornament, angels, two, glass, circa 1910, silver, minor flaking. $175
Ornament, apple, large, yellow and pink. $45
Ornament, apple, pink glass. $75
Ornament, apple, pressed cotton, early 20th century, German. $25
Ornament, apple, small. $50
Ornament, apple, yellow and red. $50
Ornament, auto, die cut. $150
Ornament, baby buggy, silver, Dresden, flat. $150
Ornament, baby in sack with purse, glass. $75
Ornament, baby in sack, glass. $45
Ornament, baby, cotton batting. $50
Ornament, baby, glass, circa 1910, excellent condition. $75
Ornament, ball with pink and gold wire-wrapped glass. $55
Ornament, ball, wire wrapped, silver with red indent, large. $75
Ornament, balloon with indents and die cut scrap angel, glass. $175
Ornament, balloon, hot air, with doll, red crochet. $75
Ornament, balloon, metal, hot air, small. $35
Ornament, balls on three arms, red, blue, gold, fantasy glass. $110
Ornament, balls, fantasy, red, blue, and gold, glass. $125
Ornament, banana, glass, circa 1920, tiny chip on top under cap. $65
Ornament, banana, unsilvered, glass, worn condition, 3½ inches. $40
Ornament, basket of flowers, blown glass, circa 1910, red, blue, and gold paint,
2½ inches long. $45
Ornament, basket, fish, small, glass. $65
Ornament, beads, glass, rope, multicolored, early 20th century, Czechoslova-
kian. $35
Ornament, bear with stick, gold, Dresden. $125
Ornament, bear with stick, white glass. $125
Ornament, bell with ball and eagle, red glass. $75
Ornament, bell with gold ball, glass. $35
Ornament, bell, fantasy with indents, glass. $110
Ornament, bell, "Merry Christmas," glass. $35
Ornament, berry, blown glass, circa 1910, some green paint left, 2½ inches
long. $50
Ornament, bicycle, cotton batting. $175
Ornament, bird cage, Dresden. $125
Ornament, bird in birdcage. $125
Ornament, bird, blue and gold with spun glass wings, hanging, glass. $95
Ornament, bird, flying with spun wings, glass. $85
Ornament, bird, milk glass, circa 1920, some pink paint remains, 3¾ inches
long. $40
Ornament, birdcage, tin, early 20th century. $22
Ornament, blue bird, clip-on, glass. $65
Ornament, boat, die cut scrap, blue glass. $175
Ornament, bottle, cotton batting. $75
Ornament, boy clown, glass, gold, circa 1910–1920, near mint. $65
Ornament, boy dressed in checked shirt, celluloid. $35
Ornament, boy in a nightcap, glass, circa 1910, near mint. $110
Ornament, boy in blue, composition. $75
Ornament, boy wearing red jacket and cap, glass. $125

Ornament, boy with die cut scrap face, cotton batting. $175
Ornament, boy with red pants, small, glass. $75
Ornament, boy's head with silver turban, glass. $95
Ornament, boy, chubby, glass with pink trim. $125
Ornament, boy, dressed in blue pants and cap, bisque. $75
Ornament, boy, patriotic, on red and white spike (top repair), glass. $95
Ornament, boy, snow, cotton batting. $175
Ornament, bug on pink daisy, glass. $55
Ornament, butterfly, clip-on, composition spun glass wings. $175
Ornament, butterfly, glass, circa 1910, yellow, red, and white with spun wings, one antennae broken, otherwise near mint condition. $125
Ornament, butterfly, two-sided, glass. $65
Ornament, candelabra, glass, circa 1890, one candle missing. $75
Ornament, candle cup, red glass. $35
Ornament, candle cup, white glass. $25
Ornament, candle, clip-on, glass. $55
Ornament, carrot, cotton batting, circa 1890, no ribs, reddish orange, near mint. $125
Ornament, carrot, glass. $100
Ornament, carrot, pressed cotton, tinsel wire wrapped, early 20th century. $28
Ornament, cat and fiddle, glass. $125
Ornament, cherub head with gold hair, glass. $125
Ornament, child with purse, pink and blue glass. $75
Ornament, child with tree, cotton batting. $175
Ornament, child, cotton batting. $65
Ornament, children, snow, pair, in white fur, movable eyes. $550/pr
Ornament, Christmas card, die cut. $35
Ornament, clown and begging dog, glass, circa 1910, excellent condition. $225
Ornament, clown bust with small green hat, glass. $50
Ornament, clown bust, red glass. $50
Ornament, clown bust, red hat, green ruffle, glass. $65
Ornament, clown bust, white glass. $35
Ornament, clown face, glass, circa 1910, "Judy," tiny chip on top at fastener. $110
Ornament, clown head on spike, red and white glass. $75
Ornament, clown head with gold cap, painted face, glass. $75
Ornament, clown head with red hat, glass. $50
Ornament, clown head, red, white, and blue hat, glass. $55
Ornament, clown head, unsilvered white with red and yellow tin clip, 5½ inches. $450
Ornament, clown, jumping jack, wood. $350
Ornament, clown on ball, double-faced, glass. $75
Ornament, clown on gold ball, double-sided, glass. $75
Ornament, clown on green ball, glass. $50
Ornament, clown on stump with accordion, glass. $45
Ornament, clown with banjo, glass. $45
Ornament, clown with blue drum, red glass. $50
Ornament, clown with red and gold dots, glass. $50
Ornament, clown with red body and silver head, glass. $50
Ornament, clown, "My Darling," red glass. $95

Ornament, clown, blue, red, and silver, glass. $60
Ornament, clown, red and gold with purple trim, glass. $60
Ornament, clown, silver glass. $45
Ornament, cuckoo clock, glass. $55
Ornament, cop, glass, circa 1910, with annealed legs, minor tarnishing. .. $75
Ornament, cornucopia with flowers, unsilvered, wire-wrapped white glass.
.... $55
Ornament, cornucopia, purple paper, Dresden. $75
Ornament, cornucopia, velvet. $45
Ornament, cracker, gold foil. $35
Ornament, diamond shape, die cut. $25
Ornament, dog in a sack, "My Darling," green glass. $85
Ornament, dog on ball, glass. $125
Ornament, dog with horns (devil dog), cotton batting. $175
Ornament, dog, composition. $25
Ornament, dog, rust glass. $35
Ornament, dog, Scottie, yellow glass. $75
Ornament, doll head, glass, blue, circa 1900, some flaking. $65
Ornament, doll in colonial purple outfit, bisque head, feet, hands. $250
Ornament, doll with brown and yellow embossed dress, china. $95
Ornament, doll, bisque with real hair. $75
Ornament, doll, boy, dressed in dark red velvet. $95
Ornament, doll, china with red and white print dress, lace trim. $85
Ornament, doll, composition, with white dress and red trim. $75
Ornament, Dresden alligator (restored). $350
Ornament, Dresden angel with blue skirt, flat. $75
Ornament, Dresden angel, flat. $65
Ornament, Dresden angel, red and gold, large. $125
Ornament, Dresden automobile pop-out. $35
Ornament, Dresden automobile, gold pop-out. $40
Ornament, Dresden baby buggy, silver. $135
Ornament, Dresden basket of fruit, flat. $100
Ornament, Dresden bi-plane. $775
Ornament, Dresden bird (one wing), gold. $150
Ornament, Dresden birdcage, flat. $75
Ornament, Dresden buffalo. $250
Ornament, Dresden bug, flat. $135
Ornament, Dresden camel. $50
Ornament, Dresden cat (ear restored). $575
Ornament, Dresden child with wreath, flat. $160
Ornament, Dresden duck (foot repair). $225
Ornament, Dresden elephant. $65
Ornament, Dresden elephant, silver. $400
Ornament, Dresden ewer, silver. $395
Ornament, Dresden fish, flat. $80
Ornament, Dresden fish, red mouth, small. $80
Ornament, Dresden flower basket, flat. $100
Ornament, Dresden flower with star in center. $50
Ornament, Dresden flower, flat. $60
Ornament, Dresden fox. $225
Ornament, Dresden frog, sitting. $150
Ornament, Dresden frog squatting, small, pink. $175

Ornament, Dresden frog with big mouth, sitting. $150
Ornament, Dresden geometric (open filagree). $75
Ornament, Dresden geometric, flat. $75
Ornament, Dresden gold cross, large. $150
Ornament, Dresden harp, flat. $40
Ornament, Dresden horse in silver saddle, flat. $100
Ornament, Dresden jockey on horse, green. $395
Ornament, Dresden lobster, flat. $160
Ornament, Dresden lyre, brown with tinsel. $75
Ornament, Dresden lyre, gold paper lace trim. $60
Ornament, Dresden moose. $375
Ornament, Dresden mythological figure, flat. $85
Ornament, Dresden owl. $275
Ornament, Dresden pig (ear restored). $375
Ornament, Dresden pistol. $300
Ornament, Dresden polar bear. $400
Ornament, Dresden poodle with top hat and glasses. $550
Ornament, Dresden rabbit, small. $150
Ornament, Dresden ram, white. $350
Ornament, Dresden rooster, white. $350
Ornament, Dresden sailboat with flag, flat. $100
Ornament, Dresden sailboat, flat. $85
Ornament, Dresden Santa, large, mesh bag. $165
Ornament, Dresden Santa in sleigh. $75
Ornament, Dresden sheep. $65
Ornament, Dresden shoe, high-button, brown. $375
Ornament, Dresden shoe, high-button, silver. $400
Ornament, Dresden shooting star, embossed, two-sided. $45
Ornament, Dresden shooting star, flat. $35
Ornament, Dresden spur, silver. $275
Ornament, Dresden stork. $325
Ornament, Dresden sun face. $600
Ornament, Dresden vase, flat. $100
Ornament, ear of corn, glass. $65
Ornament, egg, red, silver and blue, glass. $35
Ornament, end-of-day on pike, glass. $55
Ornament, fantasy with six arms, glass. $75
Ornament, fantasy, red, gold, silver bells, glass. $95
Ornament, Father Christmas, gold tree, clip-on, glass. $85
Ornament, Father Christmas, red, 5½ inches. $200
Ornament, Father Christmas, white, 11½ inches. $700
Ornament, Father Christmas, white, 8 inches. $500
Ornament, Father Christmas, white, 9½ inches. $550
Ornament, figure with green pants, pink, green, white shirt, cotton. $55
Ornament, finials, blue silvered with tin base and screw fastener. $35
Ornament, fish with tail, small, glass. $50
Ornament, fish, chips at end and hanger incomplete, 2¾ inches. $10
Ornament, flower on yellow bowl, wire-wrapped glass. $110
Ornament, Foxy Grandpa, glass, circa 1900 with annealed legs, minor tarnishing. $250
Ornament, gauze with skater. $25
Ornament, Germany, 1920s, blown glass Happy Hooligan clip-on (in fine original condition), height 4½ inches. $375

Ornament, Germany, 1920s, blown glass policeman clip-on (in fine original condition), height 4 inches. $225

Ornament, girl in skirt and apron, cotton batting. $175

Ornament, girl with basket, cotton batting. $175

Ornament, girl with doll, cotton batting. $175

Ornament, girl with opera glass, cotton batting. $200

Ornament, girl's bust in flower, glass, circa 1900, silver with green leaves, excellent condition. $125

Ornament, girl's head on bell, glass. $75

Ornament, girl, chubby, glass with pink trim. $125

Ornament, girl, red, fat, glass, circa 1900, excellent condition. $125

Ornament, girl, with cat, die cut and cotton batting. $200

Ornament, glass bead, star shape, early 20th century. $65

Ornament, glass, circa 1930, parsnip face, silver with blue, red, black, light flaking. $75

Ornament, gold fish with tail, glass. $85

Ornament, grape cluster, glass. $35

Ornament, Happy Hooligan, clip-on, glass. $150

Ornament, horn, tin, early 20th century. $25

Ornament, horse, glass, circa 1910, mercury, free-blown, some tarnishing. $125

Ornament, hot air balloon with die cut scrap angel, wire-wrapped pink glass. $175

Ornament, hot air balloon, crochet (purple) with two dolls. $85

Ornament, house with two arms, fantasy, glass. $100

Ornament, house, milk glass, circa 1920, most red and green paint remains, excellent condition, height 2½ inches. $75

Ornament, icicle, large, glass. $50

Ornament, icicle, pressed cotton, early 20th century. $25

Ornament, icicle, tin, 16 pieces, in box, early 20th century. $15

Ornament, Indian head on clip, with painted decoration, early 20th century. $450

Ornament, Indian, standing, glass, circa 1920, annealed legs, silver with red, black, and yellow, light corrosion, 5½ inches long. $100

Ornament, Joan of Arc, glass, circa 1910, glass eyes, excellent condition. $95

Ornament, Keystone Cop head, glass. $125

Tinsel-covered ornament in the form of a gramophone. COURTESY OF SALLIE AND BOB CONNELLY.

Ornament, Keystone Cop, glass, circa 1910, annealed legs, silver with gold, red, blue, and brown, light corrosion and darkening, 4¾ inches long. $90

Ornament, Kugel, bunch of grapes, blue, unsilvered, 4¾ inches high. ... $615

Ornament, Kugel, glass, circa 1890, blue, corrosion on fastener and splitting, otherwise very good condition, 2-inch diameter. $150

Ornament, Kugel, glass, circa 1890, gold, tarnishing, very good condition, 1¾-inch diameter. $35

Ornament, Kugel, glass, German, circa 1880, gold, near mint with minor tarnishing, 6-inch diameter. $250

Ornament, Kugel, glass, grapes embossed gold, late 19th century, German. $200

Ornament, Kugel, glass, pear shape, silver, late 19th century, German. . $200

Ornament, Kugel, light green, 4¾-inch diameter. $200

Ornament, Kugel, silver with hanger on each end, 4-inch diameter. $100

Ornament, Kugels, three, circa 1900, two dark blue, one green, tarnishing and one cap replaced, very good condition, approximately 2¼-inch diameter. $325/all

Ornament, lady, Victorian, die cut scrap, cotton batting. $150

Ornament, ladybug, glass. $75

Ornament, lantern with candle, hard plastic, mid-20th century. $10

Ornament, lantern, milk glass, circa 1920, a little green paint remaining, 2½ inches long. $35

Ornament, lantern, paper, handpainted, Japanese, doll size. $15

Ornament, lion tennis player, milk glass, circa 1920, original peach, brown, red, silver, and black paint remains, 3¼ inches long. $175

Ornament, Little Mermaid, McDonald's, in original box, contemporary. ...$3

Ornament, Little Miss Muffet, glass, circa 1930, silver with red, black, pink, and gold, darkening on face, light flaking, 3¼ inches high. $125

Ornament, Little Red Riding Hood head, glass, circa 1910, blown glass eyes, traces of red and flesh-colored paint, 2⅝ inches long. $110

Ornament, Little Red Riding Hood, glass, circa 1900, glass eyes, yellow and silver, near mint. $125

Ornament, man in moon, pink and gold glass. $85

Ornament, man on horse, composition. $175

Ornament, mandolin, glass. $75

Ornament, Mary Pickford, glass. $375

Ornament, monkey, glass. $250

Ornament, mushroom, glass. $25

Ornament, oak leaf with pine cones, blown glass, circa 1910, red paint and glitter left, 2⅞ inches long. $150

Ornament, old man, milk glass, circa 1920, some red, blue, and green paint remaining, 2⅞ inches long. $100

Ornament, owl, clip-on, glass. $60

Ornament, owl, pink on body, unsilvered, white glass. $45

Ornament, owl, silver and red glass. $35

Ornament, Palmer Cox Brownie, glass (hole in ears). $150

Ornament, Palmer Cox Brownies, circa 1890s, set of five. $700/set

Ornament, parasol, blue, opened, unsilvered, wire wrapped with Dresden stars, glass. $125

Ornament, parasol, closed, gold, unsilvered, wire-wrapped glass. $100

Ornament, parasol, open, lace trim, wire wrapped, pale blue, glass. $135

Ornament, parasol, open, white with red tassle, wire wrapped, glass. $100

Ornament, parasol, paper, folding, handpainted, Japanese, early 20th century, miniature size. $12

Ornament, parasol, unsilvered, blue, white, wire wrapped, glass. $125

Ornament, parasol, wire-wrapped white glass. $100

Ornament, parrot, gold and silver with angel hair tail, tin clip, 7 inches. . $35

Ornament, pea hen, clip-on, glass. $50

Ornament, peach, blown glass, circa 1910, original red-and-peach-colored paint, 2½ inches long. $35

Ornament, peach, fuzzy, glass. $75

Ornament, peacock with spun tail, glass. $75

Ornament, pear with die cut scrap bird, wax covered, glass. $95

Ornament, pear with face, glass. $125

Ornament, pear, painted, unsilvered glass. $35

Ornament, pickle, glass. $75

Ornament, pig, pink glass. $145

Ornament, pig, silver, glass. $145

Ornament, pig, two-sided, paper. $30

Ornament, pine cone, blown glass, circa 1910, original blue paint, 2½ inches long. $125

Ornament, pine cone, glass, clip-on, circa 1910, excellent condition. $95

Ornament, plum, milk glass, circa 1920, original red-and-peach-colored paint, 2 inches long. $50

Ornament, Popeye, glass, circa 1930, silver with red, black, white, and brown, some corrosion and darkening, 5¼ inches long. $125

Ornament, purse with red and white daisy, wire wrapped, glass. $75

Ornament, rabbit, clip-on. $65

Ornament, rabbit eating carrot, glass. $75

Ornament, reflector, marked ''Germany,'' circa 1890s, tin lead alloy geometric, excellent condition. $5

Ornament, roly-poly, red and blue glass. $45

Ornament, roping glass bead, four strands, each strand approximately 100 inches long, minor damage. $130

Ornament, rose, clip-on, glass. $65

Ornament, rose with leaf, clip-on, white glass. $55

Ornament, rose, blown glass, circa 1910, traces of pink paint, 2⅛ inches long. $100

Ornament, Santa and bells, die cut scrap, wire-wrapped balloon, pink glass. $175

Ornament, Santa and child, die cut scrap, wire-wrapped pink glass. $150

Ornament, Santa Claus, lithographed paper embossed with spun glass. ... $75

Ornament, Santa Claus, lithographed paper with cotton batting. $175

Ornament, Santa Claus, Victorian, crochet, cloth, and celluloid. $75

Ornament, Santa face on cone (moon), glass, circa 1900, red, white, and silver, minor tarnishing. $100

Ornament, Santa face on pine cone, glass, circa 1900, excellent condition. $125

Ornament, Santa in sleigh, glass. $75

Ornament, Santa on ball, glass. $65

Ornament, Santa, die cut scrap with wire-wrapped swan boat, glass. $150

Ornament, Santa, die cut scrap, cotton batting. $125

Ornament, Santa, die cut scrap, wire-wrapped hot-air balloon, pink, large, unsilvered, glass. $175

Ornament, Santa, glass, long, red, circa 1890, excellent condition. $85

Ornament, Santa, holding tree, glass, circa 1900, excellent condition. $125

Ornament, Santa, large, red glass with gold tree. $110

Ornament, Santa, large, white glass with glitter trim. $75

Ornament, Santa on clip, glass, circa 1910, red and silver, excellent condition. $95

Ornament, Santa on clip, glass, circa 1910, tarnishing. $75

Ornament, Santa on leaf, pink, silver, glass. $85

Ornament, Santa on pine cone, glass, circa 1900, red rope, white and blue background, excellent condition. $100

Ornament, Santa, silver and pink clip-on, glass. $75

Ornament, Santa wearing blue pants, cotton batting. $150

Ornament, Santa with arms folded, clip-on, red glass. $110

Ornament, Santa with axe and tree, pressed cotton. $250

Ornament, Santa with black mustache, red glass. $75

Ornament, Santa with child, die cut. $225

Ornament, Santa with clip, glass, gold, circa 1920, near mint, height 3½ inches. $95

Ornament, Santa with three children, die cut. $225

Ornament, Santa, blown glass, circa 1910, silver, red, and green, excellent condition, 3½ inches long. $100

Ornament, Santa, carved, jumping jack, 19th century. $325

Ornament, Santa, sleigh and reindeer, die cut scrap. $160

Ornament, Santa, small, pink glass with green tree. $60

Ornament, Santa, small, red, blue pants, green tree, glass. $75

Ornament, Santa, with clip, glass, circa 1900, minor flaking, height 5 inches. $65

Ornament, school bell, pastel red, white, and blue glass. $25

Ornament, scrap, circa 1900, paper tinsel and cotton, full-color lithograph of Santa carrying toys, advertises a grocer in Erie, PA, excellent condition, with a few pencil lines, height 9 inches. $150

Ornament, Shiny Brite, box of 12, mid-20th century. $35/all

Ornament, shooting star, glass. $65

Ornament, snake, silver glass. $45

Ornament, snake, glass. $35

Ornament, snake, red and silver glass. $45

Ornament, snow child, green glass. $100

Ornament, snow-man figure, cotton batting. $75

Ornament, snow man with accordion, glass. $45

Ornament, snow man with children, glass. $75

Ornament, snow man with green hat and broom, glass. $65

Ornament, snow man with pink hat and silver broom, glass. $65

Ornament, snow man with red hat, glass. $65

Ornament, snow man, milk glass, circa 1920, has some orange, red, and blue paint left, 3 inches long. $45

Ornament, snow man, pressed cotton with glitter trim, early 20th century, German. $15

Ornament, snow man, white glass. $25

Ornament, snowflake, Gorham, sterling silver, 1973. .... $65

Ornament, soccer player, cotton batting. $135

Ornament, squirrel eating a nut, small, glass. $75

Ornament, star and moon, cotton batting. $125

Ornament, star with blue and silver leaves. $75

Group of early 20th-century tinsel and die cut ornaments. COURTESY OF
JOAN AND ALLAN LEHNER.

Ornament, star, beaded. $55
Ornament, stocking, mesh. $45
Ornament, stork (baby), cotton batting. $35
Ornament, stork with black legs, large, glass. $75
Ornament, stork, clip-on, glass. $65
Ornament, stork, large, silver glass. $95
Ornament, swan boat with die cut scrap angel, wire-wrapped pink glass.
.... $175
Ornament, swan boat with paper sail, white glass. $150
Ornament, swan boat, unsilvered, pink wire-wrapped Santa, die cut scrap, glass.
.... $175
Ornament, swan, wire-wrapped pale blue glass. $125
Ornament, swan, with spun glass wings and tail, circa 1900, excellent condi-
tion. $150
Ornament, teddy bear, early 20th century, Germany, blown glass, standing white
bruin wearing boots, height 4½ inches. $160
Ornament, teddy bear, glass. $350
Ornament, teddy bear, yellow glass. $175
Ornament, tinsel and die cut scrap. $35
Ornament, top, unsilvered white and gold, glass. $75
Ornament, tree top, blown glass angel, late 19th century, silvered, fair condi-
tion. $55
Ornament, tree top, blown glass star, late 19th century. $75

Group of late 19th- and early 20th-century Christmas ornaments.
COURTESY OF SALLIE AND BOB CONNELLY.

Ornament, tree top, glass point, circa 1900. .... $35
Ornament, tree with red garland, glass. $75
Ornament, tree, clip-on, gold glass. $75
Ornament, tree, clip-on, gold balls, large, glass. $95
Ornament, tree, clip-on, pink glass. $75
Ornament, tree, clip-on, silver glass. $75
Ornament, tree, clip-on, red and silver glass. $75
Ornament, trolley, cotton batting. $250
Ornament, turkey, glass, circa 1900–1910, minor tarnishing. $75
Ornament, umbrella, large, closed, glass. $50
Ornament, vase with die cut flower, wire-wrapped white glass. $125
Ornament, vase with indents and berries, wire-wrapped pink glass. $150
Ornament, vase, blue and pink flower, wire-wrapped glass. $110
Ornament, wheelbarrow, tin. $75
Ornament, witch head on clip, glass. $150
Ornament, wreath, painted metal. $35
Ornaments, birds, four, glass, circa 1910, two little ones marked "Germany,"
two birds on clips, excellent condition. $125/lot
Ornaments, birds, seven, glass, circa 1920, including four song birds, two cock-
atiels, one parrot, silver with reds, blues, yellows, and blacks, a couple of feet
need to be reglued into bodies, light corrosion, littlest bird's tail is inside it.
....$100/all
Ornaments, birds, six, circa 1890–1920, four with clips, one peacock, one owl,
minor flaking. $250/all
Ornaments, birds, six, Germany, circa 1890–1920, four with clips, one owl,
one blown hanger, minor tarnishing and flaking. $275/all
Ornaments, birds, six, glass, clip-on, circa 1930s, one needs legs glued back
on, silver with red, green, blue, and black, minor flaking, fine to excellent
condition. $150/all
Ornaments, birds, two, glass, circa 1910, minor tarnishing. $75/2

Ornaments, blown glass, four, circa 1900–1910, including poinsettia 2⅜ inches long, scrolled bulb 2½ inches long, lantern 2⅝ inches long, small oak leaf 2¼ inches long, some red paint on each. $210/4

Ornaments, candlesticks, two, glass, circa 1910, one has glass bunch of grapes on bottom, other is oval rose. $175/2

Ornaments, Dresden, late 19th century including bicycle, bat, stork, alligator, dachshund, goat, and two small fish, together with a plaster pumpkin ornament. $1,200/all

Ornaments, Dresden, late 19th century, comprising a woman horseback rider jumping a fence, a fish, dog, rabbit candy container, a camel carrying trunks, a dove, and a shotgun, together with an ornament of a wooden handcarved donkey. $1,200/all

Ornaments, Dresden, late 19th century, including a balloon, two fish, a kangaroo, a lion, and an elephant's head, together with ornaments including a cigar candy container, a bottle, two canvas butterflies, and a metal tennis racket. $800/all

Ornaments, Dresden, late 19th century, including a bi-plane, a bat, an oil tank truck (lacking back wheels), a giraffe, a turkey, and a quarter moon, together with a metal tennis racket and four cherub ornaments. $800/all

Ornaments, Dresden, late 19th century, including a lock and key, a fish, lobster, poodle, lion, reindeer, and a star, together with a group of ornaments including a hat candy container, bottle, two large canvas butterflies, and two small canvas butterflies. $800/all

Ornaments, Dresden, late 19th century, including a quarter moon depicting a man, a horseback rider, parrot, lobster, monkey on a branch, and a hand gun, together with a miscellaneous group of ornaments including a cotton Santa Claus, a cotton figure, a clown, five canvas butterflies, four birds, seven modern metal ornaments. $800/all

Ornaments, Dresden, late 19th century, including a star, horseback rider, rooster, two goats standing on a barrel, and a fish, together with a lute candy container and a group of wooden implements including an ox, a spade, golf club, three oars, hay fork, harpoon, shepherd's staff, and a mortar board. $1,200/all

Group of late 19th- and early 20th-century blown glass Christmas ornaments. PRIVATE COLLECTION.

Ornaments, Dresden, late 19th century, including an elf riding a deer, sun, tiger, bird, polar bear, fox, and two fish, together with a metal tennis racket. $1,200/all

Ornaments, Dresden, late 19th century, including bicyclist on a velocipede, swordfish, doe, bull, shotgun, and a French horn, together with three other ornaments including a wooden camel, a cigar, and a heart candy container. $1,200/all

Ornaments, Dresden, late 19th century, including mandolin, turtle, cockatoo, and an artist's palette, together with a miscellaneous group of ornaments including a cotton batting clown, an elephant, cowboy on horse, skeleton, three modern metal ornaments, a large canvas butterfly, two small canvas butterflies, and three cloth birds. $800/all

Ornaments, Dresden, late 19th century, including pair of ice skates, man riding a horse, zebra, and peacock, together with a group of ornaments including a pipe candy container, German helmet, cotton batting snow man, metal tennis racket, two small canvas butterflies, a large canvas butterfly, four modern metal ornaments, a plaster figure, and a papier-mâché container. $800/all

Ornaments, glass and paper, circa 1930s, including ten paper whirl-glo cups, 2 inches high, five pins, four pins and a glass Christmas top, 10½ inches high, silver, pink, and white, excellent condition. $65/all

Ornaments, glass, circa 1930, including three horns and a cello, silver with red, green, blue, and purple, flaking, otherwise fine condition, 3 inches to 4 inches long. $125/all

Ornaments, glass, eight, circa 1910, including one cotton batting ball, four pieces of fruit, one wreath with heart, one umbrella, one balloon with wire, minor flaking and wire loose on balloon. $150/all

Ornaments, group of 39, late 19th and early 20th centuries, German, blown glass. $250/all

Ornaments, group of 37, late 19th and early 20th centuries, German, blown glass. $150/all

Ornaments, group, and light bulbs, late 19th and early 20th centuries, blown glass; Santa, horn, shoe, two birds, two tadpoles, 17 assorted sphericals; carved wooden angel, 32 assorted tree lights (some lot wear and damage). $50/all

Ornaments, late 19th and early 20th centuries, blown glass, including Santa, dirigible, birds; light bulbs; lanterns, Santa head, dirigible with American flag; and cardboard candy container of Santa in a red-flocked suit and a fur beard (damage to lot). $100/all

Ornaments, late 19th and early 20th centuries, including nine blown figural tree ornaments: potato, parasol, bird, baby, basket, barrel, bead cross; silver tinsel and bead tree top and a box of small ornaments (some lot damage and paint loss). $150/all

Ornaments, late 19th century, German, cotton, including two Santa Clauses, a clown, a Pierrot, a girl holding a mallet, two girls and a Chinese man, together with a group of 15 flags, four birds, three butterflies, and seven modern metal ornaments. $700/all

Ornaments, lot of late 19th/early 20th century, including eight blown figural ornaments: airship, ladybug, snow man, bird, house, coffee pot, basket, kite man; box with mostly musical instruments; box of 12 Italian ornaments, some damage and paint loss. $100/all

Ornaments, lot, early 19th/early 20th century, including eight blown figural ornaments: basket, Santa, bird, bell, clown, frosted airplane, etc.; six glass icicles and a box of small ornaments, damage and paint loss to lot. $100/all

Group of blown glass Christmas ornaments and bulbs. COURTESY OF
GARTH'S AUCTIONS.

Ornaments, lot, for Christmas tree, late 19th/20th century, blown glass, clip-on
and hanger-type, owls, peacocks, parrots, penguins, and many others in various
shapes and sizes (some paint flaking and repainting). $150/all
Ornaments, Santa, box of 12, plaster, 3 inches tall. $75/set
Ornaments, Santa, eight, cotton batting, circa 1920, minor wear and dirt, height
of the tallest is 2½ inches. $50/8
Ornaments, Santas, three, glass, circa 1920, minor flaking. $50/3
Ornaments, two, late 19th/early 20th century, a Dresden full-bodied elephant,
ivory-colored with tusks, and a brown bear candy container with glass eyes.
.... $200/all
Paper dolls, Dolls of Christmas, London, boxed, early 20th century. $150
Pen wipe, green and red felt with bells attached. $35
Pin, holly and berries, enamel on sterling, 1930. ....$50
Pin, Santa Claus on chimney, composition, early 20th century. $45
Pin, Santa Claus, hard plastic, Jingle Bells, 1950. ....$25
Plaque, wall, Santa, molded and painted paper, Germany, 25 inches tall.
....$135
Plate, Bing & Grondahl, Christmas 1922, Star of Bethlehem. $50
Plate, Bing & Grondahl, Christmas 1972, in Greenland. $30
Plate, Bing & Grondahl, Christmas 1987, Christmas Remembered. $50
Plate, Bing & Grondahl, Denmark, 1915. ....$125
Plate, Bing & Grondahl, Denmark, 1964. ....$50
Plate, Bing & Grondahl, Denmark, 1971. ....$15
Plate, Bing & Grondahl, Denmark, 1981. ....$35

Group of mid-20th-century Christmas candy containers, Kewpie plate, and decorations. PRIVATE COLLECTION.

Plate, Goebel, Heavenly Angel, 1971. .... $600
Plate, Gorham, Partridge in a Pear Tree, 1970. ....$125
Plate, Gorham, Rockwell Christmas Series, 1974. .... $25
Plate, Holly Hobby, Christmas 1974. .... $15
Plate, Kewpies, Christmas 1973, Cameo Productions, Japan. $125
Plate, Leyendecker, Santa Loves You, 1977. .... $45
Plate, Rockwell, Bringing Home the Tree, 1970. ....$125
Plate, Royal Copenhagen, Christmas 1951. .... $200
Plate, Royal Copenhagen, Christmas 1962. ....$175
Plate, Royal Copenhagen, Christmas 1965. .... $40
Plate, Royal Copenhagen, Christmas 1971. .... $35
Plate, Royal Copenhagen, Christmas 1981. .... $25
Plate, Royal Copenhagen, Denmark, Christmas 1951. ....$325
Plate, Royal Copenhagen, Denmark, Christmas 1960. .... $75
Postcard, boy with presents, Frances Brundage, early 20th century, embossed
cardboard. $10
Postcard, child with Christmas tree, house in background, early 20th century.
....$7
Postcard, Christmas winter scene, hold-to-light, early 20th century. $35
Postcard, Kewpies next to tree, signed Rose O'Neill, early 20th century, em-
bossed cardboard. $35
Postcard, Santa Claus smoking pipe seated in chair, early 20th century. ... $10
Postcard, Santa Claus with mistletoe wreath, early 20th century. $10
Postcard, Santa in auto, movable wheels, early 20th century, German. $50
Postcard, Santa in car, filled with gifts, German, early 20th century. $18
Postcard, Santa Claus, embossed cardboard, German, 1920s. $5
Print, cover from *Harper's Weekly*, Christmas 1883, printed in black and red,
framed, 21 1/4 inches × 17 1/4 inches. $25
Print, Santa Claus in sled delivering toys. $20
Prints, framed, three, a cracker-scrap Santa and sleigh, another of Santa on a
mule, and a print of Santa ready to descend a chimney. $25/all
Puzzle, Santa Claus, Aunt Louise's Cube, McLaughlin, 1884. .... $35

Christmas lithographed puzzle in original box. COURTESY OF MARY AND BOB
SCHNEIDER.

Puzzle, Santa Claus, three paper lithograph puzzles, framed and matted, Milton
Bradley, early 20th century. $125
Puzzle, wooden Christmas card, 1930, "Seasons Greetings." $18
Reflector, foil-covered cardboard, geometric shape, early 20th century, Ameri-
can. $5
Reflector, foil-covered cardboard with tinsel wire, early 20th century, German.
.... $10
Reflector, foil-covered paper, early 20th century. $5
Reflector, tin, early 20th century. $5
Santa, and animals, circa 1900–1910; 11 lambs and one goat: three lambs,
wooden with coats; three papier-mâché, four bisque, marked "Germany," one
stick-leg, marked "Germany"; one cast-iron goat; Santa marked "Germany";
largest lamb has one ear chipped, otherwise all excellent, some minor flaking,
tallest is 5 inches. $100/all
Santa, and sack, printed cardboard, circa 1930, red and white, fine condition,
with hanger, height 5 inches. $12
Santa, and sleigh, celluloid, circa 1930, red and white, near mint, 10½ inches
long. $125
Santa, banner, printed cotton, early 20th century, "Merry Christmas, Happy
New Year." $250
Santa, chenille on cardboard base, pipe-stem body, early 20th century. $35
Santa, chromoliths, two, color, framed, early 20th century. $90/2
Santa, composition, circa 1890, red coat, purple pants, black boots, minor cracks
at clay feet (from drying), near mint, unlisted, height 13½ inches. $375
Santa, composition, Germany, circa 1920, original packages in wood sled, one
tip of runner broken and glued, some flaking on boots, otherwise near mint
condition, 6 inches × 12 inches. $450
Santa, composition, possibly German, circa 1910, faded red cloth robe, black
boots, beard is shedding, minor flaking, nice early Santa. $450

Early 20th-century Santa figure.

COURTESY OF JOAN AND ALLAN LEHNER.

Santa, cotton batting, circa 1880s, cotton white body, scrap paper face, red scrap buttons, mint condition, height 10 inches. $200

Santa, display, circa 1920s, mechanical, turns and waves his arm, very good condition, height 5 feet. $800

Santa, early 20th century, Germany, all papier-mâché, fully jointed head and limbs, flannel outfit, height 17 inches. $1,800

Santa, early 20th century, Germany, papier-mâché and cloth, molded and painted face, hands, and feet, rabbit fur mustache and beard, red flannel outfit (feather tree missing, condition good), height 10¾ inches. $375

Santa, early 20th century, Germany, papier-mâché and cloth, molded and painted head, hands, and boots, white rabbit fur mustache and beard, blue-gray flannel hat and great coat with black curly wool trim, carrying wicker basket (Christmas tree missing, good condition), height 10⅜ inches. $950

Santa, German, early 20th century, seated figure having papier-mâché face, hands, and boots, rabbit fur beard, red and white felt hooded coat and blue pants, very good condition, height 7¼ inches. $200

Santa, German, early 20th century, seated, with papier-mâché face, hands, and boots, rabbit fur beard, red and white felt hooded coat and blue pants, evergreen branch, height 7¼ inches; red and green painted wooden sled, length 13¼ inches, width 4½ inches, height 4½ inches. $450

Santa, group of five, die cut, framed, 9 inches × 12 inches. $25

Santa, in a plane, pressed cardboard, circa 1910, few small edge tears, 11 inches wide. $75

Santa, in rattan sleigh, early 20th century, sitting figure with papier-mâché head, hands, and boots, fur beard, wood and wire body, red felt top and blue pants, height 7½ inches, sleigh wound with red ribbon (damaged), length 9¼ inches. $185

Santa, in sled, milk glass, circa 1900, two pieces, traces of gold remain, 4¼ inches × 5 inches. $125

Santa, in sleigh, celluloid, Japan, 1930s, carrying large sack, sleigh pulled by two deer, metal traces, one smaller deer, overall length 18 inches. $125

Santa, in wooden sleds and Santa candy container, 20th century, Germany and Japan, cloth and wire figures with papier-mâché face, hands, and boots, one in a painted sled, length 5½ inches, two in a natural wood sled, length 5 inches; small Santa stands beside a snow-covered brick house, 6¾ inches × 8 inches. $275/all

Santa, Japan, mid-20th century, papier-mâché, molded and painted figure wearing red outfit trimmed with white chenille, black boots, carries pack basket filled with tree, toys, and goodies, two Christmas balls over his arm, minor wear, height 11 inches. $200

Santa, labels, paper, framed, marked "Germany," circa 1900, colorful lithograph, frame is new, Santas are original and in excellent condition. $35

Santa, marked "Japan" on base, circa 1930, composition red suit, blue pants, black boots, excellent condition. $35

Santa, mask face, circa 1920, some wear, flaking on belt, small dents on face, slight darkening, height 27 inches. $100

Santa, mask face, circa 1930s, cute musical wind-up, reddish-brown suit with black belt and boots, white bag, excellent condition, could be cleaned, height 10¼ inches. $25

Santa, mid-20th century, cloth and papier-mâché, electrified, molded and painted head, head nods and mouth opens and closes, cloth body and limbs, synthetic fur-trimmed red velvet outfit, Converse rubber Mickey Mouse boots (rubber alligatored, general fabric wear, mechanism needs rewiring), height 36 inches. $80

Santa, mid-20th century, German, all wood, probably a store display, stylized figure, a cloth sack over shoulder, carries switches in one hand and gifts in the other, height 40 inches. $160

Santa, on skis, circa 1930, red coat, gray pants, black boots, excellent condition, height 4 inches. $50

Santa, on sled, wood and cloth, painted bisque face, fur beard, runners glued, 5¼-inch length. $95

Santa, pull toy, composition and reindeer, Germany, circa 1890, antlers missing on reindeer, straps broken under stomach, otherwise near mint, length 9⅞ inches. $300

Santa, seven-piece lot, 20th century, including seated Santa in white cardboard sleigh pulled by pair of white celluloid deer with bells and ribbon reins, three standing Santas, composition Santa squeaker, snow man and snowball candy boxes (minor damage to lot). $200/all

Santa, three items, 20th century; five-figure Santa metal candy mold, length 10½ inches; stamped tin-and-wood figural noisemaker, height 4¾ inches; lithographed paper-on-wood jumping jack, height 8¾ inches (some lot wear). $150/3

Santa, wood cut, Thomas Nast, 1878, double-page book illustration with full typography on reverse, Santa in fur at left of fireplace, jester figure on right displaying year 1878 on chest, 13½ inches × 20⅜ inches. $250

Santa Claus, and feather tree, 1930s and 1950s, branches tipped with berries or candle holders, square base with stenciled detail, height 44 inches; papier-mâché face (slight paint wear), cloth body and limbs over a wire armature, red velvet suit with plush trim, lambskin beard, height 19¾ inches. $175

Santa Claus, bisque face, occupied Japan, 4 inches. $35

Santa Claus, full figure, plastic, 1950s. $10

Santa Claus, German, papier-mâché, early 1900s, the figure with painted facial features and a white beard, wearing a red wool coat and blue felt pants with black composition boots, the composition and wire body allows the figure to be in a seated position, height 13 inches. $750

Santa Claus, red plush over wire, circa 1940, 3½ inches. $20

Santas, composition, circa 1890, three German, two on sleds, one on bench, very good to excellent condition, tallest is 3½ inches. $400/all

Santas, seven, bisque chalk and soapstone, circa 1920s, little one marked "Germany," some wear, sizes range from 1½ inches to 3 inches. $200/all

Santas, six, bisque and chalk, circa 1920s, red, feet glued on one Santa, some flaking and tiny chips on the rest. $150/6

Santas, six, circa 1920, one celluloid, near mint, five composition and cotton batting, minor wear. ...., ... $225/6

Santas, three, circa 1900, one papier-mâché, wax coated, two wax Santa candles, near mint. ....: $100/3

Santas, three, papier-mâché, the whole Santa is near mint, the other two have some wear and a few tiny holes, height of tallest is 10 inches. $250/3

Seals, Christmas, 1940s, package. $5

Sheep, six, composition, circa 1910, one has a dark brown coat, minor flaking and darkening, height of tallest is 3½ inches. $175/6

Sheet music, Irving Berlin, "White Christmas." $25

Sled, Santa Claus, cast-iron miniature, late 19th century, scroll runners, name in raised letters on top (weld repair, traces of paint), length 5½ inches. ... $100

Sleigh, Santa, cardboard, and two celluloid reindeer, Japanese, circa 1930, fine condition, Santa 5 inches high, sleigh 6½ inches long. $75

Snow babies, bisque, seated on box, Germany, 2 inches. $200

Snow babies, bisque, standing, Germany, 2½ inches. $200

Snow babies, Christmas figures, cast-metal dog sled team and Eskimo boy, early 20th century, most marked "Germany," polar bears, babies, and elves on sleds, skiing, skating, and nodding Santa (minor wear and paint loss). $600/all

Snow baby, bisque, figure on sled, Japanese. $125

Snow baby, bisque, figure on top of polar bear, marked "Germany." $150

Snow baby, bisque, figure with glitter, large size. $125

Snow baby, bisque, figure with skis, Japan. $35

Snow dome, Santa Claus, plastic base. $20

Snow dome, snow man, plastic base, mid-20th century. $15

Spoon, Christmas design, sterling silver and enamel. $75

Spoon, Danish, Michelson, enamel and silver, 1960. .... $45

Spoon, demitasse, sterling silver, Santa Claus, chimney, and fireplace. $50

Spun glass, rosette, central flower, tinsel wire wrapped, die cut angel. $75

Spun glass, rosette, die cut scrap of cherub, single-sided. $45

Stocking, celluloid toys, red net, mid-20th century, Japanese. $25

Stocking, chromolithographed paper, early 20th century, German. $250

Stocking, mid-20th century, mesh with toys, original condition. $30

Stocking, printed fabric cut and sewn into the shape of a stocking, Saint Nicholas laden with toys on one side and smiling moon over city buildings on reverse, with first verse of *T'was the Night Before Christmas*, length 30 inches. ... $130

Stocking, stencils of Santa, sleigh, roof, red, white, mid-20th century, Japanese. $15

Stockings, three, late 19th century, full color, cotton, two illustrating Santa going down the chimney, the third shows stockings hung on the mantel and child in bed frame, 34¼ inches × 22 inches. $600/3

Tablecloth, printed paper, Santa in sleigh with toys and reindeer, original cellophane package. $15

Tea set, child's, china with decal decoration, original box. $100/set

Tea set, child's, German china, decal scenes depicting Santa in balloons, zeppelins, and autos. $450/set

Textiles, apron, half, organdy with applied berries and mistletoe, early 20th century. $35

Textiles, apron, printed cotton with Christmas motifs, mid-20th century. .. $20

Textiles, bib, embroidered "Baby's First Christmas," mid-20th century. $5

Textiles, seven, and two feather-style trees, late 19th/early 20th century; hand-kerchiefs: Nash Santa Claus, Grandfather's Clock illustrated song, Skip Rope; sewn Christmas stockings and Palmer Cox China man, sailor, and German, slight fading; trees have stenciled wooden bases, heights 10⅝ and 12⅞ inches; cotton flannel and fur, poodle height 14 inches (some lot wear). $250/all

Textiles, suspenders, satin, handembroidered holly and berries, early 20th century. $125

Textiles, tablecloth, damask with printed holly and mistletoe leaves, with eight napkins, circa 1920. ....$75/all

Textiles, tablecloth, printed cotton Santa and stockings, mid-20th century. $35

Tin, toffee, English, 1930, lithograph, Santa with children. $25

Toy, blocks, Christmas scenes lithographed. $100

Toy, blocks, Santa Claus and teddy bear, German, original box. $750

Toy, roly-poly Santa, painted papier-mâché, early 20th century, 8 inches tall. $125

Toy, Santa, celluloid head, tin, wind-up, rings bell, original box, mid-20th century, Japanese. $50

Toy, Santa Claus on scooter, battery operated, original box, mid-20th century. $150

Toy, Santa Claus on sled, celluloid face, tin wind-up, made in Japan, mid-20th century. $75

Toy, Santa Claus with drum, battery operated, mid-20th century, Japanese. $75

Toy, Santa in auto, lithographed tin friction toy, Japanese, minor rust, 5½-inch length. $100

Toy, Santa mechanical, tin with celluloid head, made in Japan, mid-20th century. $75

Toy, Santa on polar bear, papier-mâché, 12 inches. $175

Toy, slipper-sleigh, red paint, black and gold outlining, circa 1900. ......$500

Toy, wind-up Santa and sleigh, tin and plastic, polychrome paint, some cracks, mid-20th century, 8-inch length. $20

Toy, wind-up Santa on reindeer, tin, cloth, and plastic, working condition, mid-20th century, Japanese, 5¾ inches high. $25

Tree, aluminum, mid-20th century, 4 feet high. $65

Tree, bottle-brush, mid-20th century, Japanese, 5 inches high. $3

Tree, bottle-brush, snow-covered, mid-20th century, Japanese, 3 inches high. $2

Bottle-brush Christmas trees.
COURTESY OF JOAN AND ALLAN LEHNER.

Tree, bubble light, circa 1950, green, artificial, with 11 bubble lights on it, working, excellent condition, height 17 inches. $55

Tree, cardboard, metal bells on branches, German, early 20th century. ...$250

Tree, cellophane needles with bubble lights. $75

Tree, cellophane, white, early 20th century, 25 inches high. $95

Tree, feather, and 50-piece miniature Nuremberg village, late 19th/20th century, tree with red berries stands in red turned wooden base, height 18 inches; painted village has eight buildings, 20 carved animals, people, trees, fence, etc., some damage and paint loss. $200/all

Tree, feather, glass icicles, beads, and ornaments, early 20th century, 5 feet high. $500

Tree, feather, mid-20th century, Germany, U.S. zone, square wooden base with stenciled holly decoration (few berries missing from end of branches), 38 inches tall. $175

Tree, feather, musical tin base, early 20th century. $350

Tree, feather, reproduction, small size. $38

Tree, feather, white, early 20th century, 18 inches high. $300

Tree, feather, with wooden base, circa 1930, in original box, a couple of branches are loose, excellent condition, height 67 inches. $65

Tree, fiberglass, mid-20th century. $35

Tree, goose feather, large, with Victorian ornaments, mounted on a revolving music-box stand, surrounded with a wood and metal ornamental fence, a church scene, and a nativity. $750

Tree, goose feather, miniature, with glass ornaments. $125

Tree, green chenille, original box, 1920, 7 feet high. $300

Tree, green feather with a few red berries and tin candle sockets, turned wooden base, old white paint, worn condition, 22½ inches high. $25

Tree, green feather with red berries and tin candle sockets, turned wooden base with old white paint, marked "made in Germany," 39 inches high. $200

Tree, green feather with red berries, turned wooden base, old white paint, marked "Germany," very worn condition, 20 inches high. $35

Tree, green feather, turned wooden base with old white paint, brown paper-wrapped stem, wire branches with red berry ends, some wear, 31 inches high. $100

Tree, green feather, wooden base with old red paint, brown paper-wrapped stem and wire branches with red berry ends, berries are worn, 68 inches high. $300

Tree, green fiber, red wooden base and green paper-wrapped stem, 47 inches high. $25

Tree stand, cast iron, patent applied for North Bros. Manufacturing Co., with threaded color, old gold and black paint, 10 inches high. $35

Tree stand, cast iron with embossed bark and knots, old black and gold paint, 7¼ inches high. $75

Tree stand, cast iron, bells and scroll work. $65

Tree stand, cast iron, red and green wreath, early 20th century. $75

Tree stand, cast iron, Santa's head and beard in relief, original red, green, and gold paint, 11-inch diameter. $265

Tree stand, Father Christmas, cast iron, Germany, early 20th century, 8 inches tall. $125

Tree stand, German, late 19th century, musical. $500

Tree stand, iron, molded cherubs, painted, made in Germany, minor rust, 7 inches tall. $75

Group of early and mid-20th-century village buildings with mica decorations. COURTESY OF JOAN AND ALLAN LEHNER.

Tree stand, iron, molded poinsettias. $35
Tree stand, Noma Santa decals, circa 1930, 11 inches tall. $75
Tree stand, Santa and sleigh, painted tin, early 20th century. $150
Tree stand, wooden, early 20th century, German. $40
Village scene, cardboard, fencing and buildings, mid-20th century. $75/all
Village scene, 15 buildings, wooden, electrified with sleighs and trees, early 20th century. $2,500/all
Village scene, house, cardboard with glitter, 1940s. $15
Village scene, lot of 13 paper buildings, painted and glitter, mid-20th century. $125/all
Wall decoration, Santa, sleigh, brown reindeer, Germany, embossed cardboard, 10 inches. $40
Wall hanging, Santa with pack of toys, handpainted canvas, signed "Children of Grade 3, Public School 27," 1940. .... $100

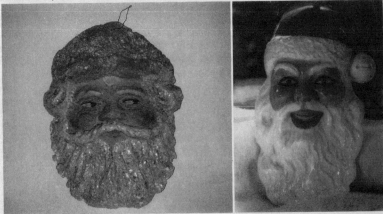

Left, *early 20th-century embossed cardboard wall decoration with mica trim.* COURTESY OF DON MEHRER. Right, *early 20th-century wall decoration in the form of Santa's head.* COURTESY OF JOAN AND ALLAN LEHNER.

Late 19th-century framed black-and-white Christmas and New Year's woodcut, $250. COURTESY OF SKINNER AUCTIONS.

Wall hanging, Santa, handpainted, made for Macy's, New York, 1930s, depicting a standing Santa talking on the phone, on velveteen (violet fabric faded to a pleasing puce shade), 87 inches × 48 inches. $500

Wall hanging, Santa, handpainted, made for Macy's, New York, 1930s, depicting full-size seated Santa reading a list, on velveteen (violet fabric faded to a pleasing puce shade), 87 inches × 48 inches. $350

Wax, angel, flying, molded legs and arms, cardboard wings, early 20th century, German. $125

Wax, angel, spun glass dress, blown glass eyes, German, early 20th century. $175

Wax, angel, spun glass wings, cardboard body, fabric skirt and mohair wig, German, 1940. ....$125

Wax, Baby Jesus, small, in cardboard manger. $35

Wreath, bog moss, berry and ribbon trim, doll-house size, late 19th century, American. $95

Wreath, bottle-brush wire with fabric ribbon, "Merry Christmas," miniature. $15

Wreath, chenille, electrified. $35

Wreath, felt holly leaves with composition berries, homemade over wire frame, 12-inch diameter. $35

Wreath, pressed paper, electrified twinkling light, mid-20th century, Japanese. $25

Wreath, Santa in wreath, plastic, electrified, mid-20th century, 26-inch diameter. $65

Minor Holidays

There are a number of holidays celebrated in the United States for which there seem to be no apparent decorations. For example, Groundhog's Day, February 2, brought to the United States by German and English settlers, was used to forecast the weather for the next six weeks. If the groundhog appeared on that day and his figure cast a shadow, one could expect six more weeks of winter.

February 12 was the original date for Abraham Lincoln's birthday. Observance of his birthday has been replaced by the national observance of President's Day (see The Patriots chapter).

Memorial or Decoration Day, originally observed on May 30, honored the Civil War dead. Later, the day became a memorial to all war veterans and is now celebrated with parades and the marking of graves by replanting them and by the placing of wreaths on war memorial statues.

Legend says that Betsy Ross created the first U.S. flag on June 14, now known as Flag Day.

Labor Day was first celebrated on September 5, 1882, in honor of America's working class. This holiday continues to be celebrated on the first Monday of September, usually with parades and picnics.

Bunting, usually in red, white, and blue, and flags are the only known decorations for some of these aforementioned holidays.

Celebrations

Even though there may not be a specific market for decorations and memorabilia for many of the following special occasions, they nevertheless merit inclusion in a book about holidays and their celebrations because most of the items mentioned were first used in the early part of the twentieth century and are, when found, considered collectible. They, like almost all of the other holiday ornaments, decorations, and party favors, were not thought important enough to save for future generations to use and enjoy. We suggest that you begin to look for these items in your family's attic.

Birthdays

Birthday party or christening celebrations called for specialized items such as crowns, horns, table decorations, plates, napkins, cups, nut cups, place cards, invitations, greeting cards, banners, imprinted balloons, favors which were baked into the cake, decorative candles, tablecloths, gift wraps, party hats, and table favors.

To commemorate the birth date, one can find zodiac spoons in sterling silver made by Gorham, Wallace, and Kirk in the first quarter of the twentieth century. Storks, Mother Goose, cats, bunnies, dogs, and wise old owls were some of the prominent motifs used to record birthdays. Flower-of-the-month and day-of-the-week spoons, as well as records of the birth month or day were also made in sterling silver or 14 karat gold, occasionally set with jewels. The handles were full-figure caricatures engraved with lines from the nursery rhyme: "Monday's child is fair of face; Tuesday's child is full of grace; Wednesday's child is full of woe; Thursday's child has far to go; Friday's child is loving and giving; Saturday's child works for its living; and a child that's born on the Sabbath Day is fair and wise and good and gay."

Sweet Sixteen

For this very special occasion in a young girl's life, printed paper goods such as table decorations, tablecloths, plates, napkins, cups, nut cups, place cards, invitations, party favors, and greeting cards, including those with caricatures, were manufactured. Oftentimes they were sugary, sweet, and in pastel colors, usually decorated with festoons of floral swags and/or ribbon bow knots. Corsages made from sugar cubes tied with tiny satin ribbons were often worn by the birthday girl.

Engagements, Weddings, and Anniversaries

A full range of commercially produced paper products, usually in white and silver, was available to commemorate these important occasions. Included were centerpieces featuring wedding rings and doves, paper flowers, honeycomb wedding bells, paper streamers, and wedding cake tops, place-card holders, invitations, embossed cardboard boxes for holding the wedding cake, full-figure Cupids with doves, swags, and floral sprays, paper plates, tablecloths, napkins, cups, nut cups, greeting cards, and decorative molded candles. In the 1930s, the Dennison paper company offered a complete wedding party of cardboard dolls dressed in crepe paper gowns and tuxedos.

Wedding and Baby Showers

Crepe paper full-figure swans or love boats were common symbols used

Early 20th-century wedding figures.
RIVATE COLLECTION.

as a table centerpiece or other decoration for wedding showers. Crepe paper flowers on wire stems filled flower pots or silver-covered boxes for decorating the table. Chandeliers were covered with silver paper shades from which were suspended satin ribbons with hearts and flowers. In addition, full-figure umbrellas, either homemade or rented from the Dennison party store, were covered with crepe paper and ribbons and often had a surround of metallic cellophane simulating raindrops. Most of the printed tablecloths were checkered paper with pressed cardboard cherub silhouettes at each corner. Matching pieces often included invitations, place cards, nut cups in the form of swans or cherubs, paper plates, napkins, cups, and decorative molded candles.

Baby shower decorations in either pink or blue were printed with bouncing babies, storks or nursery rhymes. Table centerpieces in pressed cardboard were in the form of storks, cradles, and perambulators with babies.

Graduation

Matching paper products imprinted with graduates in cap and gown, the mortar board or diploma motifs included invitations, party hats and favors, paper plates, napkins, tablecloths, cups, nut cups, greeting cards, and full-figure candles. The wise old owl, a symbol of knowledge, was also often used as a table centerpiece or an imprinted motif.

During the late nineteenth century, sterling silver spoons were made to honor the graduate. The spoons had handles with full figures attired in cap and gown. Specific colleges, such as Harvard, the University of Missouri, and others, issued spoons. In 1902, the first sterling spoon to honor the girl graduate was produced.

Theme Parties

During the early part of the twentieth century it was common to host costume parties, and not just at Halloween. Imaginative creations were conceived by the inventive party goer. Many of these costumes are being resurrected, reassembled, and worn to today's parties. Common themes for the parties were pirates, Hawaiian, Hollywood, and the Mardi Gras. Paper goods to carry out the Hawaiian theme, for example, would have been imprinted in tropical colors with splashy palm trees, native flowers, pineapples, and dancing native couples. Paper leis, purchased from the party store, were given as favors. Women guests were expected to dress in native costumes, often the traditional grass skirts. Men carried bongo drums, the common musical instrument. Party booklets gave further explicit directions for transforming one's home, fraternity or sorority house into a fantasy island complete with related recipes such as ambrosia for transporting one to an island of dreams.

In the early part of the twentieth century, Disney themes began to be used for children's parties. A complete line of party goods was available to ensure the success of these parties also.

Celebration Listings

Birthdays

Child, birthday cake candle holders, figural kittens, pressed wood, handpainted, mid-20th century, package. $10/pkg

Child, birthday cake candle holders, pastel flowers, molded composition on original cardboard, 1940, package. $10/pkg

Child, Birthday Zoo, animals in cages printed on paper plates and cups, circa 1940. .... $5

Child, candle, figural number one. $3

Child, candle, figural number one decorated with baby motifs, early 20th century. $5

Child, centerpiece, Bambi, pressed cardboard with tissue fold-out base, 1940. .... $15

Child, centerpiece, cake with circus animals, cardboard, color lithographed, 1920. .... $15

Child, centerpiece, clown, tissue paper fold-out with cardboard base, mid-20th century. $10

Child, centerpiece, fire engine, cardboard, full figure, movable wheels, early 20th century, homemade. $35

Child, centerpiece, locomotive, interlocking printed cardboard with engineer, 1940. .... $10

Child, centerpiece, pirate's treasure chest, cut-out cardboard, filled with cardboard coins, early 20th century. $35

Child, centerpiece, Raggedy Ann and Andy, cardboard, tissue paper fold-out, mid-20th century. $35

Child, centerpiece, Sesame Street, Big Bird, crinkled crepe paper over wire frame, cardboard feet, mid-20th century. $30

Child, centerpiece, Snoopy, crepe paper and cardboard, 10 inches high, mid-20th century. $20

Child, ceramic plate, plays "Happy Birthday," 1940. .... $15

Child, favor, hat, fire chief, molded cardboard, opens to fill with candy, early 20th century. $35

Child, favor, loot bag, lithographed paper, "Happy Birthday," mid-20th century. $3

Child, game, Pin the Tail on the Donkey, laminated fabric, early 20th century, original box. $35

Child, game, Twister, contemporary. $2

Child, garland, foil-covered cardboard cut-out "Happy Birthday," early 20th century. $3

Child, invitation, cowboy party, lithographed paper, early 20th century, group of three. $5/3

Child, invitation, Peter Pan and Wendy, homemade, paper, early 20th century. $5

Child, napkins, clown holding balloons, in original cellophane package, mid-20th century. $3/pkg

Child, noisemaker, horn, coated cardboard, crepe paper ruffle, early 20th century. $3

Child, noisemaker, whistle blow-out, lithographed paper cardboard and feather, early 20th century. $5

Child, nut cup, crepe paper-covered cardboard with puppies in basket and name tag. $5

Child, nut cup, double crepe paper frill with cut-out Mickey Mouse and name tag. $10

Child, paper doll, Dolly Dingle's Birthday Cards for all the family, uncut, early 20th century. $15

Child, party hat, cone shape, colored cardboard with feather plume and sparkles, early 20th century. $3

Child, party hat, crown, Burger King, mid-20th century. $5

Child, party hat, crown, mica-covered cardboard, early 20th century. $5

Child, party hat, fire chief, cardboard, red, homemade, early 20th century, fair condition. $20

Child, party hat, Mouseketeer ears, mid-20th century. $15

Child, party hat, tissue paper with ribbon trim, early 20th century. $3

Child, place card, ballerina dance party, lithographed paper, set of 12. ....$15/set

Child, place card, clown cut-out, cardboard, colored, mid-20th century. $3

Child, snappers, crepe paper covered with ribbon ties, multicolored, box of 12, early 20th century. $50/box

Child, snappers, pink crepe paper covered with gummed flower sticker decoration, water stained. $2

Child, streamers, pastel printed "Happy Birthday," Dennison, crepe paper, early 20th century. $5

Child, tablecloth, cowboy and Indian motif, printed paper, early 20th century. $5

Child, tablecloth, Mickey Mouse, with stamped border, paper, early 20th century. $15

Child, tablecloth, Sesame Street, Big Bird, printed paper, original package, mid-20th century. $5

Nut cup, basket, hard plastic, decorated with fabric flowers, mid-20th century. $6

Sweet sixteen, corsage, sugar cubes tied in pink satin ribbons, fair condition, 1940. .... $15

Sweet sixteen, hat, crown, silver-covered cardboard, glitter decoration, 16 in center, 1930. ....$5

Sweet sixteen, invitation, birthday cake, 16 candles, printed paper, package, 1940. .... $5/pkg

Sweet sixteen, streamers, pink and silver crepe paper, 32 feet long, 1940. ..$5

Sweet sixteen, tablecloth, napkins, and matching plates, pink and white printed paper "Sweet 16" and rose border, Dennison, 1930, package, fair condition. $18/all

Births and Christenings

Book, birth record, pink leather, embossed gold baby, early 20th century. $10

Book, moiré covered, baby on cover, dated 1932. ....$5
Candy container, baby shower, stork, cotton. $22
Candy container, baby shower, stork, cotton batting over paper, wire legs, wood beak, blown glass eyes, early 20th century. $125
Candy container, baby shower, stork, glass eyes, molded cardboard, Japan, 1930. ....$40
Candy container, baby shower, stork, glass eyes, papier-mâché, large size. $225
Candy container, baby shower, stork, papier-mâché, Germany, early 20th century. $110
Candy container, baby, nude, pressed glass, with original candy and tin cap, early 20th century. $55
Candy container, Kewpie, bisque, dressed as baby, standing on circular cardboard box, early 20th century. $175
Candy container, stork with baby, cardboard, mid-20th century. $45
Candy container, stork, papier-mâché, box opens under wing, 1930. .....$125
Centerpiece, cradle, pressed cardboard with crepe paper flowers, Dennison, 1930. ....$50
Centerpiece, stork, pressed cardboard, holding baby in flannel wrap, pipe cleaner legs, 1940. ....$35
Centerpiece, umbrella, printed crepe paper with pink and blue bows and flowers, and pink and blue fringe crepe paper border, 1940. ....$25
Cup, christening, embossed cherubs, sterling silver, American, 19th century. $150
Cup, christening, embossed rococo scrollwork, English, sterling, 1893. ..$175
Dress, christening, batiste, lace and cut work trim. $75
Dress, christening, cotton smocking and embroidery, early 20th century. .$125
Favor, baby, celluloid, wrapped in pink blanket, 2 inches, early 20th century. $18
Favor, cradle on cardboard rockers, satin ribbon and floral bouquet, 1940. ..$7
Favor, cradle, filled with netting and candy, hard plastic, mid-20th century. $5
Favor, stork, pipe cleaner with crepe paper frill, early 20th century. $10
Invitation, baby shower, handpainted watering can, dated 1932. ....$3
Invitation, baby shower, stork holding baby, lithographed paper, 1930, package. $5/pkg
Mold, chocolate, baby sucking thumb, tin, early 20th century. $150
Mold, chocolate, stork, tin, early 20th century. $45
Nut cup, crepe paper-covered cardboard with paper umbrella on handle, 1930, Japanese. $10
Nut cup, crepe paper double frill, with cut-out baby and name tag, dated 1925. ....$5
Place card, baby shower, pipe cleaner stork with clothing, early 20th century. $5
Tablecloth, frolicking babies and raindrops, early 20th century, printed paper in cellophane package. $10/pkg
Tablecloth, stork with baby and ribbon border, paper, Dennison, with matching napkins and cups. $25/all

Graduation

Candle, girl graduate, 1940. ....$5
Centerpiece, owl, cardboard, seated on book of knowledge, 1940. ....$25

Favor, cardboard mortar board with candy insert, 1935. ....$5
Favor, college pennant, felt, miniature size, 1930, Harvard. $5
Invitation, rolled-up diploma, paper, 1930. ....$3
Nut cup, crepe paper-covered cardboard, cut-out mortar board on name tag.
....$5
Tablecloth, girls and boys in caps and gowns, printed paper, original cellophane
package, 1930. ....$10/pkg

Theme Parties

Hawaiian, centerpiece, crepe paper tropical flowers with palm fronds in wooden
bowl, 1940. ....$22
Hawaiian, centerpiece, palm trees and grass hut, papier-mâché and cardboard,
homemade, 1935. ....$35
Hawaiian, centerpiece, pineapple, molded cardboard, tissue paper fold-out
crown. $25
Hawaiian, centerpiece, volcano, cardboard, 1930. ....$10
Hawaiian, costume, grass skirt, paper lei, fabric bra, 1930. ....$35
Hawaiian, costume, sarong, printed floral bark cloth fabric, 1930. ....$35
Hawaiian, decoration, bongo drums, cardboard, painted decoration, 1930.
....$20
Hawaiian, favors, leis, paper, 1930, package. $10/pkg
Hawaiian, invitation, palm tree and full moon, handpainted paper, 1930. ...$5
Hawaiian, menu, ''Luau,'' handpainted palm trees, pen and ink menu. ... $10
Hawaiian, wall decoration, palm tree, cut-out cardboard, Dennison, 1935.
....$15
Mardi Gras, crown, Rex, 1915. ....$10
Mardi Gras, devil costume with papier-mâché mask, 1930. ....$35
Mardi Gras, favor, scepter, cardboard, 1930. ....$5
Mardi Gras, invitation, costume parade, 1940, printed paper. $3
Mardi Gras, invitation, mask, cut-out cardboard, early 20th century. $3

Mardi Gras mask depicting Stan Laurel, early 20th century, papier-mâché. COURTESY OF SANDWICH AUCTION.

Mardi Gras, noisemaker, horn, lithographed tin "Mardi Gras." $10
Mardi Gras, noisemaker, rattle, tin with lithographed paper depicting revelers, 1930s. $7
Mardi Gras, souvenir, vase, black amethyst glass, silver overlay, New Orleans, 1934. .... $22
Pirate, centerpiece, galleon, cardboard, tissue paper sails, 1930. .... $35
Pirate, centerpiece, treasure chest, lithographed cardboard, filled with jewelry and coins, 1930. .... $25
Pirate, costume, Captain Kidd, head scarf, gold earring, eye patch, knee britches, black boots with gold buckle. $35
Pirate, favor, bottle of rum, crepe paper-covered cardboard. $5
Pirate, favor, treasure chest, lithographed cardboard, lift-top with hinge, water damaged, 1940. ....$5
Pirate, game, Treasure Hunt, missing pieces, in original box, early 20th century. $5
Pirate, invitation, "Hunt For Sunken Treasure," March 1927. ....$5
Toga party, costume, cloth toga, sandals, crepe paper-covered laurel wreath on wire frame, 1940s. $10
Toga party, invitation, Roman Coliseum, pen and ink on paper, 1935. ......$5
Toga party, photograph, 1940, University of Illinois, fraternity party. $5

Wedding

Basket, flower girl, sterling filigree, late 19th century, original satin ribbons. $150
Basket, flower girl, white wicker with ribbon-wrapped handle, 1930. ...... $10
Box, wedding cake, cardboard embossed with doves and ribbons, circa 1940. .... $15
Box, wedding cake, cardboard lithographed with wedding bells, mid-20th century. $8
Cake top, 25th anniversary, heart frame with silver bells on cardboard base, early 20th century. $25
Cake top, bisque bride and groom figures, lacking veil, set in wire heart form, circa 1920. .... $25
Cake top, bisque full-figure bride and groom, Edwardian costume, 8 inches high. $95
Cake top, bisque Kewpie figures dressed as bride and groom, early 20th century. $125
Cake top, soldier in uniform and bride, on circular disk with flower border, 1940s, fair condition. $35
Candle, bride and groom, mid-20th century. $10
Candle, swan, mid-20th century, small size. $5
Candy box, Bible form, white with attached gilt wedding ring, mid-20th century. $12
Candy box, white cardboard, sprig of artificial orange blossoms and ribbon trim, early 20th century. $10
Candy container, heart-shaped cardboard with white wedding bells on lid, early 20th century. $35
Candy container, wedding cake shape, tiered, cardboard, early 20th century. $50
Candy container, white satin-covered cardboard with full-figure dove and wedding ring, mica trimmed, early 20th century. $45

Centerpiece, table, bridal shower, watering can, pressed cardboard covered with white crepe paper and cellophane water drops, homemade, 1930. .... $35

Centerpiece, table, Cupid, full figure, molded cardboard, holding wedding rings, early 20th century. $30

Centerpiece, table, dove, honeycomb tissue paper wings on cardboard base, 12-inch diameter, 1940s. $20

Centerpiece, table, flower pot, ceramic, filled with crepe paper flowers on wire stems, Dennison, 1940. .... $25

Centerpiece, table, love boat, with portholes and lithographed floral trim on crushed crepe paper waves, early 20th century. $75

Centerpiece, table, swan, pressed cardboard with embossed feathers, 12-inch length. $35

Cookie cutter, wedding bells, tin, early 20th century. $10

Cup, wedding, silver, embossed scrollwork, mid-19th century. $350

Decoration, bridal shower, crepe paper-covered umbrella with wire frame and cellophane fringe, early 20th century, fair condition. $75

Decoration, bridal shower, wishing well, lithographed cardboard with lace and flower trim, mid-20th century, poor condition, 4 feet high. $35

Decoration, white honeycomb paper wedding bells with silver glitter, large size. $25

Doll, bride, bisque, mid-20th century, Nancy Ann Storybook, in original box. $25

Doll, bride, Madame Alexander, hard plastic, jointed body, original lace gown and veil, mid-20th century. $75

Dress, all-over lace, pleated hemline, early 20th century, stained condition. $35

Dress, handmade lace over ivory silk, high neck, long sleeves, late 19th century. $225

Dress, lace, ivory colored over slip, early 20th century. $225

Dress, silk, leg-of-mutton sleeves, narrow waist, pleated skirt, circa 1900. .... $175

Dress, Victorian, white on white lace trim, late 19th century, fair condition. $275

Dress, Victorian, cotton batiste, lace trim, tucked skirt, two-piece, boned neck with lace, small size. $75

Dress, white batiste, white embroidery, cut work inserts, Edwardian. $75

Fan, wedding, all-over lace, ivory sticks, late 19th century. $110

Favor, 50th anniversary, cardboard cake box embossed with golden bells and anniversary greetings, early 20th century. $10

Favor, bride's shoe with wedding ring buckle with net-covered candy, mid-20th century, 2½ inches. $7

Favor, cake, wedding symbols, tin, in original baking package, 1940s. $10/pkg

Favor, candy box, white silk roses on lid, stained condition, early 20th century. $10

Favor, confetti, cellophane package, tied with ribbon and orange blossom, 1920. ....$10/pkg

Favor, high-heel plastic white shoe with net insert holding almonds, mid-20th century, 3 inches. $10

Favor, tulle package containing rice, ribbon ties, homemade, 1930, faded condition. $8

Favor, two-pence coin wrapped in white netting with satin ribbon bow and orange blossom, early 20th century. $25

Garland, interlocking tissue paper, flower swag, 10 feet. $20

Garland, white and silver tissue paper, 12 feet long, early 20th century. .. $10

Handkerchief, wedding, batiste with Irish lace trim. $75

Handkerchief, wedding, white organdy, white embroidered hearts, early 20th century. ...., ... $10

Invitation, bridal shower, cut-out cardboard umbrella with handpainted flowers and raindrops, early 20th century. $12

Invitation, bridal shower, handpainted bride with floral swag, dated 1906. $10

Invitation, wedding, handpainted roses and leaves on white parchment paper, homemade, June 1916. .... $25

Kimono, wedding, red silk, embroidered cranes and pine trees, Japanese, early 20th century. $175

Menu, bridal shower, luncheon, umbrella cardboard cut-out, calligraphy, homemade, circa 1930. .... $15

Menu, wedding supper, pen and ink with handpainted flowers in corners, dated June 12, 1927. .... $25

Mold, chocolate, doves and wedding ring, tin, late 19th century. $55

Mold, ice cream, bride with long veil, hinged pewter, 1920. .... $65

Mold, ice cream, wedding bells, pewter, early 20th century. $35

Paper doll, bridal party, uncut, Whitman, 1973. .... $25

Paper doll, bride and groom, Merrill, 1949, uncut. $10

Paper plates, bridal shower, umbrellas and flowers on white paper, mid-20th century, package. $3/pkg

Paper plates, wedding bell and ribbons, printed paper, cake size, together with matching cups, 1940. ....$5/all

Parasol, white silk, Battenberg lace, wooden handle, poor condition, late 19th century. $75

Pillow, ring, embroidered satin with chenille roping, late 19th century, homemade. $35

Place card, bride and groom, lithographed cardboard, with name tag, circa 1920. ....$5

Place card, cardboard cut-out, Kewpie dressed as bride, name tag base, early 20th century. $20

Place card, dried flower bouquet with ribbon tie and name tag, early 20th century. $18

Posey holder, flower girl size, gilt metal, embossed rose motif. $375

Posey holder, sterling silver tripod, pearl decoration, circa 1860. ....$975

Posey holder, sterling silver, French, scrollwork and vines, flowers inset with turquoise. $1,200

Sheet music, "Wedding Bells Are Breaking Up That Old Gang of Mine," early 20th century. $10

Streamers, congratulations, white and silver crepe paper, 1940. ....$5

Tablecloth, bridal shower, watering cans and flowers, multicolor printed paper with package of napkins, 1940. ....$7/all

Tablecloth, bridal shower, white umbrellas on pale blue ground, paper, 1940. ....$5

Tablecloth, bride and groom running to automobile, printed paper, 1930. . $10

Tablecloth, wedding bells and doves, lithographed paper with matching package of napkins, 1940. .... $20/all

Table decoration, bride figure, crepe paper-covered wire frame with chenille arms and handpainted face on cardboard disk, early 20th century. $20

Table decoration, individual crepe paper-covered clothespin dolls on cardboard bases, dressed as bride and groom, 1920, homemade. $10

Textile, bridal garter, blue and white silk, handmade with silk rosette, late 19th century. $35

Textile, suspenders, white satin embroidered with white roses, stained condition, late 19th century, handmade. $75

Holiday Hints

Before You Buy

1. Read all the books, magazine articles, auction catalogs, museum exhibition catalogs, and other printed material pertinent to the subject of your heart's desire.

2. Visit private and dealer collections. Browse antiques shows. Attend museum exhibitions. Don't forget to ask questions and to handle objects when you are able to do so. This will help you to date the pieces and know if they are "right."

3. Look the item over very, very carefully to ensure that it is in good to excellent condition and not repaired, restored, married (combined with newer piece, color and/or decoration) or a reproduction.

4. If at an auction, attend the preview. Examine the items, again carefully. Study the catalog for references to age and condition. Speak with the auctioneer, dealers, and other collectors about what is on the sales block. Set price limits for yourself after speaking with the auctioneer about estimates and premiums. Getting auction fever is really a disease.

5. If buying through mail order, use established trade publications that have checked the references of their advertisers. Before you send your check, clarify that you want a fully detailed receipt sent with the object. Agree upon return privileges.

6. If at an antiques center, group shop or mall, you will be able to examine a vast amount of merchandise in a short period of time. Sometimes, if you are lucky, it is possible to OD on holiday collectibles. If you have questions, most managers are knowledgeable about the shop's entire stock. Centers sometimes maintain "want lists."

7. If attending mega-shows or flea markets, shop carefully. It is sometimes difficult for promoters, no matter how au courant, to keep reproductions from appearing. Often, the management maintains a computer record at the entrance to the show indicating specialities of the participating dealers. Again, don't be afraid to ask questions. When buying, do *not* leave without a detailed receipt.

8. When assembling a collection, remember that dealers can be your best source. Building a relationship of mutual trust may mean developing a lifelong friendship along with a wonderful collection of objects that you will treasure.

9. Remember that studying just one area of antiques and collectibles will give you a narrow base of information from which to work. You have to study many areas to develop your eye regarding what is appropriate for the period, what tools were used, what elements were added to decorations, and what is right or not.

10. Buy what you love—not for investment—and, above all, have fun! Good luck!

Fakes and Reproductions

It is imperative that before you start your search for holiday decorations, you go to your local library or favorite bookseller and study the books on the subject. Attend antiques shows and flea markets. Go to antiques malls and tag sales to see the availability of items. Travel to museum exhibitions to increase your own memory bank. Search out the knowledgeable dealers and collectors and speak with them. Visit collections. Remember that your best tools are your eyes and the knowledge that you are able to gain through reading and seeing numerous items and collections.

There are a number of points one should be aware of when purchasing holiday decorations and ornaments. Early Dresden ornaments, made from sturdy thick cardboard, were heavily embossed. Paint colors, today, should be soft and have some fading. Old cotton batting should be soft and should have absorbed some dirt through the years. Through seeing and handling many objects, you will learn to recognize the signs of normal wear and aging.

Collectible glass Christmas ornaments are usually lightweight and have a brittle feel. When very lightly tapped, they will have a hollow sound. If blown into a mold, the ornament will also have an outline from the joins of the mold. Detailing will be crisp and, on the better old ornaments, generally well done. The addition of silvering on the inside of old ornaments is usually even, and, if flaked, will show a few brown spots. Newer glass is usually heavier and has a very slick feel. Older ornaments will generally have some degree of paint fading, occasionally only on one side where the paint was exposed to light. Early paint will not be as garish as it is on some of the later Japanese decorations. Since red is not a very stable color, soft reds sometimes turn brown. Early blues and greens are light in feeling. During the middle part of the twentieth century, more purple, orange, and acid green colors were used. Newer ornaments may only be painted on one side, whereas the older examples are painted in the round. Sometimes the country of origin will be stamped on the cap.

Full-figure, wax Christmas tree ornaments, such as those depicting angels and the Christ Child, will have color and texture variations in the wax due to exposure to the elements. In addition, when the wax was molded, it absorbed impurities from straw and dirt.

Early glass kugels generally had a cork or wax in the neck into which wire was pulled, making them easy to hang. Late nineteenth and early twentieth century papier-mâché and cardboard Santa figures were decorated with dried bog heather, a type of material no longer available. Light gray-green in color, not like the bright green plastic made today, this early moss also appeared on Santa's carts, sleds or cars.

Older feather trees, which are made from dyed goose feathers, should have dirt and dust, such as accumulated through daily exposure, in the crevices. Remember when buying that quantities of these have been reproduced. On many full-figure, papier-mâché, Santa candy containers, the cardboard candy receptacle, even though not exposed to light, looks pristine, unused, and is thicker in depth. When in doubt, seek out a knowledgeable dealer. Also, be sure when buying to get a receipt indicating age, country of origin, if known, and full description of your purchase. The seller's name and address, and the date you purchased the item should also be on the receipt.

Papier-mâché lanterns, whether made for Christmas or Halloween, will often have burn marks because they were used with candles.

Crepe paper will soften and the colors of the trims will fade with age. Early tinsel will have tarnish marks while cellophane will usually crack from years of storage.

Handcolored valentines and Frakturs from the eighteenth and nineteenth centuries need to be examined carefully. Do not buy if the piece is framed and you cannot remove it from the frame. Older paper has a softer feel or texture because there is more rag content. Look for the watercolors to have bled through the back of the paper. Make sure the drawing is a watercolor, not a print.

Iron banks, doorstops, and books have all been reproduced. If old, expect crisp detailing, signs of wear on the bases, and soft colors indicating age on the paint. It is best to purchase these items from a knowledgeable source unless you are sure.

There are a number of other elements of which to be aware. With the increase of interest in holiday collectibles, many less valuable pieces have newer paint or decorations added so that the entire piece appears to be old. Sometimes more common examples are combined (married) to make a less valuable item more attractive. For example, the background of a pressed cardboard pumpkin with a soft, aged patina can have newer, bolder paint-decorated facial features added.

Earlier books on holiday decorations have stated that Dresdens, die cut scraps, cotton batting, and paper candy containers have not been reproduced. This is absolutely not true! Almost all types of holiday ornaments are currently being duplicated, many times from the original molds. There are innumerable sources for the willing buyer. Therefore, it is important for the collector—novice or advanced—to attend gift shows, read mail-order catalogs, and visit museum gift shops to see what is currently available in the marketplace. Unscrupulous and unknowledgeable people are buying and selling items they believe to be old but are not. Use your eyes and buy wisely.

Caveat emptor—Let the Buyer Beware! The following list illustrates the reproduction offerings from the receipt of one month's catalogs just for the Christmas collector: papier-mâché Belsnickles with and without feather trees; papier-mâché Father Christmas figures with and without switches or feather trees; wooden blocks in box with lithographed paper Victorian Christmas scenes; tapestries depicting St. Nicholas with toys and dolls; goose-feather trees in several sizes; papier-mâché St. Nicholas figures with loops for hanging; Santa Claus candy containers; cotton batting hanging and standing ornaments with scrap faces; jumping jacks; lithographed fabric toys and dolls; glass candy containers in the form of full-figure Santas; Victorian crepe paper dolls to hang from the tree; all types of cookie cutters and molds; full-figure cardboard candy containers in many forms, including rabbits for Easter.

Care, Repair, and Storage

Since there are so many natural elements that are extremely harmful to a collection of holiday ornaments and decorations, it is almost a miracle that so many have survived to the present time.

Storing antique and collectible objects in attics or cellars with extreme variations in temperatures, either too hot or too cold, causes irreparable damage. Glass or enamel will often crack. Paper and cardboard become brittle, with crease or fold lines becoming more pronounced, and develop a tendency to crumble. Defects already in the piece will only become exacerbated.

Water and moisture are extreme villains for holiday collections, especially for those items made from paper. Water washes away the color and causes paint to flake. It softens cardboard ornaments and leaves stains on them. Moisture also warps ornaments and decorations and removes trims or other embellishments that were attached by glue. Water attracts silverfish, who love to eat glue and paper, leaving destruction in their wake. Mildew grows in damp areas, leaves a dark outline or stain on paint and lacquered finishes, and creates a musty smell which is almost impossible to remove.

Silver dips should not be used on any sterling or silverplated decorations because they remove a layer of silver. Years of handpolished patina can be removed by these chemical processes. It is best to use a mild silver polish which does not contain an abrasive material and apply it with a soft toothbrush or cotton rag.

Plastic or plastic wrap, especially when exposed to light and variations in temperature, causes moisture to become trapped underneath the wrap. This causes mildew to form under the wrap and a deterioration process begins that can start with paint flaking. If temperatures are extreme, the synthetic wrap will adhere to the surface it is touching and can remove paint and other decorations from the object or cause color striations to occur. If ornaments are stored in plastic boxes or any types of synthetic fabrics, they do not breathe and will deteriorate more quickly.

Folding paper goods and fabrics leaves permanent lines which, in turn, cause cracks and tears. Laying paper flat and rolling textiles are ideal. Exposing papers or fabrics to sunlight, even for short periods of time, allows the rays to penetrate the material causing varations in color.

When cleaning holiday decorations, it is best to have a very light hand. Harsh cleaning methods damage trims and lift applied ornamentation. Feather dusters are ideal cleaning tools because cloth can actually rub dirt deeper into the seams or cracks of the objects so that it begins its process of deterioration.

Commerically made household cleaners are anathema to most antique objects. They leave a residue which builds up and cannot be removed. They can also delete entire portions of painted surfaces.

When attempting to clean or restore antique or collectible objects, remember that destroying patina can be dangerous to the health, look, and feel of most antiques and collectibles. Some dirt and age lines give character to pieces. When in doubt regarding the best remedy, always ask an expert. If you feel that you own an extremely rare ornament that needs restoration or repair, it is probably a good idea to take the piece to a professional restorer for examination and proper treatment. If you are attempting to clean items yourself, it is best to use a cotton swab with plain warm water in an unobtrusive place very carefully to see if the piece can be cleaned.

Paper goods should be stored in acid-free boxes with acid-free tissue or surrounded by all-cotton towels, sheets or rags. Glass, papier-mâché or pressed board decorations should be stored in individual boxes or cartons with separate compartments where the ornaments don't touch. Breakage often occurs when ornaments touch each other. For extremely rare decorations, a crushed layer of acid-free tissue should be used as a cushion.

How to Have
Your Holidays Year-Round

1. Lighted vitrines or display cabinets keep holiday collectibles on view, dust and moisture free, and shown to best advantage.

2. Shadowboxes made from deep frames, coffee tables with inset display space, and nineteenth-century clock cases with glass doors missing their works and in otherwise unrepairable condition make wonderful display cases for groups of extremely small objects.

3. Feather trees or wooden pyramids decorated with ornaments, a few special or many different ones, make wonderful room accents.

4. Groups of Victorian glass domes with objects on view under them serve as an excellent means of display.

5. Victorian pressed glass punch bowls, compotes on standards, and store-size cake stands with covers also show ornaments and decorations to advantage, especially those that are fragile in nature, without the danger of breakage.

6. Dining tables, buffet tables, mantelpieces, bookshelves, window ledges, and kitchen or corner cupboards—all are colorfully enhanced by the addition of jack-o'-lanterns, turkeys, hearts, Easter eggs or flags.

7. Bunting or May baskets at door or window frames are cheerful invitations for one to enter.

8. Creative outdoor decorating is fun and becoming increasingly popular. Easter egg trees or newspaper-filled plastic pumpkin trash bags add a holiday spirit to the entrance to your home. Use your imagination to create your own decorations!

9. Use the walls of your home for hanging your collection. Heart-shaped pans, turkey molds or cookie cutters with holiday motifs add spice to the kitchen or dining areas.

10. Assign a specific place in your home for your holiday collectibles. Rotate decorations as the seasons and the holidays change.

Above all, use and enjoy your treasures!

Market Trends

Holiday ornaments, favors, costumes, and other decorations are part of an emerging collectibles market that is already healthy and continuing to develop. An increasing number of books on the subject have been written. Exhibitions at museums and historical societies are continuing to expand the market.

Until the recent past, few decorations, ornaments, party favors or costumes were saved. Many of these items were made in small quantities, were stored in inappropriate places like attics or basements where they deteriorated, and are today fragile. In addition, through the years decorations have been considered "kid's stuff" and, therefore, usually thrown away after being used. Scarcity has caused prices to rise. Even though Christmas and Halloween decorations seem ridiculously high to the novice, they will probably continue to rise in price as more collectors scout for the exact same items and the supply of items continues to diminish as more people become collectors. Prices for other holiday items will probably escalate as interest in them piques.

In today's market, paper and novelty manufacturers are supplying the stores with an infinite variety of holiday decorations. It might be a good idea to purchase some of what you consider the very best of these items. If possible, buy two. Use one and save the other in its original wrapping. You may have a future collectible! A number of fast-food outlets offer holiday give-aways. Again, use one and save the other.

Store advertising placards with holiday motifs are often used for one year only. Before they are thrown away, you might want to approach the store owner or manager and secure the ad for your collection. Mail-in coupon offers for products with holiday motifs are another area of future collectibility.

Remember, however, that when collecting holiday decorations, older is always better. The newer items are fun but, since they are usually made in large quantities, they will probably not rise in value as quickly.

Appendix

Sources

Antiques Shows

Alan Boss's NY Annex at 26th Street, New York City.
Farmington Antiques Show, Connecticut.
Harrisburg Antiques Show, Pennsylvania.
Hillsboro Antiques Show, California.
Houston Antiques Dealers Show, Texas.
Irene Stella's Meadowlands Show, New Jersey.
Irene Stella's Triple Pier Shows, New York City.
Jackie Sideli's Danbuy Antiques Marketplace, Connecticut.
Margaret Brusher's Ann Arbor Markets, Michigan.
May's Brimfield Antiques Market, Massachusetts.
Miami Beach Convention Center, Florida.
Norman Schaut's Atlantic City Show, New Jersey.
Papabello's Shows, Cleveland, Ohio.
Renninger's Marketplace, Denver, Pennsylvania.
Richard Kramer's Heart of Country, Nashville, Tennessee.
Richard Kramer's Home in Indiana, Indianapolis, Indiana.
Rod Lich's One-Day Markets, Indiana and Kentucky.
Sandy Smith's Fall Antiques Show, New York City.
The Crutcher Antiques Shows at the Fairgrounds, Indianapolis, Indiana.
The Fairs at Round Top, Texas.

Auction Houses

Christie's East
219 East 67th Street
New York, New York 10021

Collector's Auction Services
P.O. Box 13732–B
Seneca, Pennsylvania 16346

Sallie and Bob Connelly
666 Chenango Street
Binghampton, New York 13901

Garth's Auctions, Inc.
2690 Stratford Road
P.O. Box 369
Delaware, Ohio 43015

Mapes Auctioneers
1600 Vestal Parkway West
Vestal, New York 13850

Richard Opfer
1919 Greenspring Drive
Timonium, Maryland 21093

Pettigrew Auction Gallery
1645 South Tejon Street
Colorado Springs, Colorado
80806

Sandwich Auction House
15 Tupper Road
Sandwich, Massachusetts 02563

Robert W. Skinner, Inc.
Route 117
Bolton, Massachusetts 01740

Sotheby's Collectors' Carousel
1334 York Avenue
New York, New York 10021

Swann Galleries
104 East 25th Street
New York, New York 10010

Theriault's
P.O. Box 151
Annapolis, Maryland 21404

Special Exhibitions

Each year at Christmas, the Metropolitan Museum of Art in New York City decorates a gigantic tree with eighteenth-century Neapolitan creche figures. The Met continues a tradition begun by the donor, Mrs. Loretta Hines Howard, who combined the German tradition of decorating Christmas trees with the custom of displaying extensive nativity scenes, which had developed in southern Germany and Mediterranean Europe.

Andreas Brown presents an exceptional display and sale of antique Christmas ornaments each year at the Gotham Book Mart, 41 West 47th Street, New York City. The shop's 12-foot Victorian Christmas tree glitters with a rare, captivating, and carefully assembled collection of vintage ornaments. In exhibition cases throughout the store's second-floor gallery, an antique Christmas ornament show-of-shows with stockings, toys, and books turns the shop into a Christmas museum.

Trade Publications

Antique Monthly
2100 Powers Ferry Road
Atlanta, Georgia 30339

Antique Review
P.O. Box 538
Worthington, Ohio 43085

Antiques & Auction News
P.O. Box 500
Mt. Joy, Pennsylvania 17552

Antiques Gazette
929 Davidson Drive
Nashville, Tennessee 37205

Antique Trader Weekly
P.O. Box 1050
Dubuque, Iowa 52001

Antique Week
Box 90
27 North Jefferson
Knightstown, Indiana 46148

Arts & Antiques Antiquarian
Box 798
Huntington, New York 11743

Collectors Journal
Box 601
Vinton, Iowa 52349

Collectors News
Box 156
Grundy, Iowa 50638

Collectors Showcase
P.O. Box 6929
San Diego, California 92106

Hobbies
10006 South Michigan Avenue
Chicago, Illinois 60605

Maine Antiques Digest
Box 358
Waldoboro, Maine 04572

Massachusetts Bay Antiques
9 Page Street
Danvers, Massachusetts 01923

New England Antiques Journal
4 Church Street
Ware, Massachusetts 01082

The Newtown Bee
Newtown, Connecticut 06470

New York Antiques Almanac
Box 335
Lawrence, New York 11559

New York Pennsylvania Collector
Drawer C
Fishers, New York 14453

Renninger's Antique Guide
P.O. Box 49
Lafayette Hill, Pennsylvania 19444

Glossary

Batting. Cotton used for decorations; also known as cotton wool in Europe.

Belsnickle. Pennsylvania German name for Saint Nicholas; adaptation of Pelz-Nicol.

Bisque. Fired, unglazed porcelain.

Candy container. A holder or box for sweets, usually figural in shape and made in two parts with a lift top.

Cellophane. Cellulose that has been finished in thin strips, used for decorations, artificial grass, and trees.

Celluloid. Predecessor of plastic.

Chenille. Velvet cord with nub used for decorations, often with wire framework.

Chromolithograph. Multicolored printed paper decoration, also known as chromos.

Cobwebs. A form of valentine wherein threads are pulled into beehive or cobweb shape.

Composition. Papier-mâché with the addition of sawdust, glue, and plaster molded into forms and then painted.

Die cut. Same as a chromolithograph; a flat lithographed paper, cut with dies.

Dresden. Paper or cardboard ornament covered or trimmed with shiny metallic paper decoration.

Ephemera. Paper memorabilia.

Father Christmas. Name used for Saint Nicholas after the Reformation.

Feather tree. Artificial Christmas tree made with dyed goose or turkey feathers.

Hold-to-light. A postal or greeting card having an inserted panel of mica or transparent material that shows through the card when it is held to strong light.

Kris Kringle. Name used for German Christkindlein, the German Christ Child.

Kugel. Late nineteenth-century, silvered blown glass ornament in round or egg shape.

Mica. Also known as isinglass, a transparent mineral.

Molded cardboard. Liquid paper poured into molds, pressed into shape, dried, and then sometimes colored.

Nodder. Figure with head usually mounted on spring in order to move or tremble.

Papier-mâché. Combination of paper pulp, glue, and fillers poured into molds, dried, and painted.

Pelz-Nicol. Figure of Christ Child, usually with switch in hand.

Putz. German name for nativity scene.

Saint Nicholas. Bishop of Myra, 4th century A.D., who began the tradition of gift giving.

Schnerenschnitte. The art of paper cutting.

Scraps. Flat chromolithographed paper, also known as die cuts and chromos.

Silverplate. Pieces manufactured from a base metal with a layer or coating of silver.

Spun glass. Thin glass fibers.

Sterling silver. Pieces marked 925 or sterling are .925 parts silver out of 1,000 with .75 parts copper.

Bibliography

Brenner, Robert. *Christmas Past: A Collectors' Guide to Its History and Decorations*, Schiffer Publishing Ltd., West Chester, Pennsylvania, 1985.

Johnson, George. *Christmas Ornaments, Lights & Decorations*, Collector Books, Paducah, Kentucky, 1987.

Lee, Ruth Webb. *A History of Valentines*, Lee Publications, Wellesley Hills, Massachusetts, 1952.

Miall, Antony and Peter. *The Victorian Christmas Book*, Pantheon Books, New York, 1978.

Rogers, Maggie and Hallinan, Peter R. *The Santa Claus Picture Book*, E.P. Dutton, Inc., New York, 1984.

Rogers, Maggie and Hawkins, Judith. *The Glass Christmas Ornament: Old & New*, Timber Press, Forest Grove, Oregon, 1977.

Russell, C.J. and The Halloween Queen. *Trick-or-Treat Trader*, a bimonthly newsletter, P.O. Box 499, Winchester, New Hampshire.

Schiffer, Margaret. *Christmas Ornaments: A Festive Study*, Schiffer Publishing Ltd., West Chester, Pennsylvania, 1984.

————*Holiday Toys and Decorations*, Schiffer Publishing Ltd., West Chester, Pennsylvania, 1985.

Snyder, Phillip V. *The Christmas Tree Book*, The Viking Press, New York, 1976.

————*December 25th: The Joys of Christmas Past*, Dodd, Mead & Co., New York, 1985.

Staff, Frank. *The Valentine and Its Origins*, Frederick A. Praeger, New York, 1969.

Stille, Eva. *Christmas Tree Decorations: A Book for Collectors and Lovers of Old Things*, Hans Carl, Nuremberg, Germany, 1983.

Whitmyer, Margaret and Kenn. *Christmas Collectibles*, Collector Books, Paducah, Kentucky, 1987.

Index